FROM THE BRIDGE
HMS Invincible

a30118 045622150b

D0682839

Previous page:
**Invincible makes a fine sight as she works up to full
speed in the Irish Sea.**
HMS Invincible *Photographic Section*

This page:
**The ship visited Australia at the end of 1983 as part of
the 'Orient Express' deployment. Note the Phalanx
CIWS mounted on the stern as a result of Falklands
experience.** *HMS* Invincible *Photographic Section*

FROM THE BRIDGE
HMS Invincible
LEO MARRIOTT

LONDON
IAN ALLAN LTD

C045622150   SK 12/9x

First published 1990

ISBN 0 7110 1940 1

Published by Ian Allan Ltd, Shepperton, Surrey; and printed by Ian Allan Printing Ltd at their works at Coombelands in Runnymede, England

All uncredited photographs were taken by the Author.

Contents

Glossary

ACR	Aircraft Control Room
ADAWS	Action Data Automated Weapon System
ADEX	Air Defence Exercise
AEW	Airborne Early Warning
ASW	Anti-Submarine Warfare
Cable	Nautical measure of distance equal to 200yd
CAP	Combat Air Patrol
CASEX	Combined Anti-Submarine Exercise
C-in-C	Commander-in-Chief
CIWS	Close-In Weapon System
CPA	Closest Point of Advance
CRT	Cathode Ray Tube
CVS	Aircraft Carrier (Support)
DFC	Designated Flying Course
EW	Electronic Warfare
FDO	Flightdeck Officer
Flyco	Flying Control/Flying Control Officer
FLYEX	Flying Exercise
GWS	Guided Weapon System
HMS	Her Majesty's Ship
Lt	Lieutenant
Lt-Cdr	Lieutenant-Commander
MEOOW	Marine Engineer Officer of the Watch
NAS	Naval Air Squadron
NCS	Naval Compass Stabiliser
nm	Nautical Mile (6,080ft)
OOW	Officer of the Watch
OUT	Officer under Training
PO	Petty Officer
POMEM	Petty Officer Marine Engineering Mechanician
PWO	Principal Weapons Officer
QHM	Queen's Harbourmaster
QM	Quartermaster
RAF	Royal Air Force
RAS	Replenishment at Sea
RFA	Royal Fleet Auxiliary
RN	Royal Navy
RNAS	Royal Navy Air Station
rpm	Revolutions per Minute
SCC	Ship Control Centre
SHAR	Sea Harrier
SHINTO	Ship's Intelligence Officer
SINS	Ship's Inertial Navigation System
SKJ	Sea King (Anti-Submarine version)
SKW	Sea King (AEW version)
SNAPS	Ship's Navigation and Processing System
STOVL	Short Take-Off/Vertical Landing
UHF	Ultra High Frequency (Radio)
VHF	Very High Frequency (Radio)
WOD	Wind over the deck

INTRODUCTION

HMS *Invincible* was the first of three similar aircraft carriers to enter service with the Royal Navy during the 1980s. At the time of their inception these ships were unique in that they were designed to carry the revolutionary Harrier STOVL fighter in addition to their prime role as ASW vessels with a complement of Sea King helicopters. This concept has now been copied by several other navies including those of Spain, Italy and India, with Japan likely to follow suit in the near future.

HMS *Invincible* has recently been completely modernised so that she now carries 20 aircraft and is equipped with the latest radars, sonars and weapons systems. The functioning of such a complex vessel and its air squadrons would need

Below:
A dramatic bow view showing HMS *Invincible* at speed.
HMS Invincible *Photographic Section*

more than this volume to describe in detail but it is hoped that the following pages will give the reader at least an insight into the day-to-day routine of a warship — as viewed 'From the Bridge'.

Before attempting to describe the operation of HMS *Invincible*, it is perhaps worth briefly describing the layout of the ship and looking at the career of the man in command, Capt M. P. Gretton MA, RN.

Externally, *Invincible* displays a clean profile, uncluttered by the many overhangs and excrescences which characterise larger conventional aircraft carriers. The long island superstructure carries the Bridge high up at the forward end and also the distinctive twin funnels which house the exhausts of the four Olympus gas turbines. Two plated masts support a variety of radio and radar equipment.

The flightdeck stretches the whole length of the ship, except for an open forecastle where the Sea Dart missile launcher is positioned, and is served by two lifts which transfer aircraft to the hangar below. There are a total of nine deck levels in the hull including the flightdeck itself which is designated 1 Deck. The hangar, with its floor on 4 Deck Level, also occupies virtually two-thirds of the internal length of 2 and 3 Decks above. Officers' accommodation and the Wardroom are right aft on Decks 2 and 5 inclusive, while Senior Rates are mostly accommodated aft on 6 Deck. The Junior Rates' accommodation is right forward, mainly on 5 and 6 Decks with some messes on 2 Deck along the port side of the hangar, and on 1 Deck inside the structure supporting the ski-jump at the bows. Machinery spaces occupy the major part of the lower levels, 7, 8 and 9 Decks, together with various stores, magazines and fuel tanks. Uninterrupted access fore and aft is only possible along passageways on 2 and 5 Decks. Most of the areas vital to the running of the ship are situated on the decks below the hangar including the Operations Room,

Communications Centre and the Ship Control Centre.

Fore and aft the ship is divided into sections, each lettered alphabetically from A to U, and each compartment is given a number within this section. Thus an officer's cabin might be designated 3T21, indicating that it is compartment number 21, in section Tango (near the stern), on 3 Deck. As each compartment bears its designation painted on the entrance, this system also enables crew members or visitors to

orientate themselves quickly in any part of the ship.

To be given command of one of the Navy's major warships is a great honour and signifies that the officer concerned has already served with distinction in previous appointments. Capt Mike Gretton, the ship's commanding officer at the time of writing this book, is no exception to this rule. Aged 42 when he assumed command of *Invincible* at the end of 1988, he had previously served as the assistant navigation officer aboard the aircraft carrier HMS *Ark Royal* between 1970 and 1972 to gain his first experience of naval air operations. Subsequently he served in several ships including the frigate *Bacchante* and gained his second command, the Type 21 frigate HMS *Ambuscade*, in 1977 at the age of 31. Before coming to *Invincible*, Capt Gretton held appointments at the Directorate of Naval Plans, the staff of Flag Officer Third Flotilla, the Directorate of Naval Recruiting and attended the Royal College of Defence Studies for a one-year course. This varied and challenging service career, coupled with time spent at Trinity College, Oxford, where he obtained his MA, has produced the man for the job.

Despit his vast experience and a position of great responsibility, he still retains an almost boyish enthusiasm for the job and is respected by his officers in whom he has an obvious and appreciated trust. In looking through this book the reader may be struck by the fact that the Captain appears to do little in the routine running of the ship. This, of course, is as it should be. A naval captain, particularly on a large ship, is provided with officers of great expertise and ability of their own and he is able to delegate much of the routine administration and handling of the ship to them, However, he always bears the ultimate responsibility for whatever occurs aboard his ship and consequently has to strike a difficult balance by being fully aware of what is happening at all times and allowing his officers to exercise their professional discretion.

Despite the weighty considerations of being in command, it is likely that Capt Gretton's main emotion was one of eager anticipation as he prepared to take his ship to sea following the completion of a prolonged series of post-refit trials . . .

Right:
Invincible's Bridge towers over two Sea Harriers parked on the forward section of the flightdeck. In the background are the twin peaks known as the Paps of Jura, one of Scotland's Western Isles.

SAILING

It is a typical summer morning in Hampshire with the last shreds of overnight mist fast disappearing, while the waters of Portsmouth Harbour are barely ruffled by a light breeze. HMS *Invincible* lies quietly alongside the North West Jetty in the sprawling dockyard and Naval Base, towering above the surrounding buildings and smaller ships. Despite the general impression of calm, closer inspection of the scene reveals considerable activity. On the jetty parties of dockyard workers are gathering and the over-looking crane is manned. The forward gangplank is being lifted and swung clear of the ship, while the after access is still in place and highway to earnest-looking sailors and civilians. The waters around the ship are host to three tugs, a couple of police launches and a number of other craft. HMS *Invincible* is about to sail.

Moving *Invincible's* 20,000 tons away from the jetty and setting course within the limited confines of the harbour will be a complex task, depending heavily on the teamwork and skill of all involved. Consequently a leaving-harbour briefing is scheduled for 0930 and will be attended by the officers and senior rates involved, together with the Captain, and this will be held in one of the three Aircrew Briefing Rooms on 2 Deck immediately below the island. Compared to smaller ships where such activities have to be conducted in makeshift space such as a dining mess, an aircraft carrier can offer properly fitted spaces with facilities such as tiered seating, display boards and a small lectern. Nevertheless, the room is crowded with

Below:
An 'Invincible' class ship alongside the North West Wall at Portsmouth Dockyard.

almost 30 officers and men as Capt Gretton enters, exactly on time, at 0930. Briefly acknowledging the assembled company he takes his seat and instructs the briefing to go ahead. In charge of the proceedings is the ship's Navigating Officer, Lt-Cdr Malcolm Dodds, who calls initially for a report from one of the ship's meteorologists. The situation is that a significant area of high pressure is building to the west of the UK and this will dominate the weather pattern for the next few days. Winds will be light northwesterly, although are expected to veer to the nor'nor'east later in the day. A layer of thin altostratus will persist for much of the day, possibly giving some very light rain. Inland, some heavy thunderstorms are expected and, as will be seen, these will have some effect on the ship's programme.

The actual plan for moving the ship out into the tidal stream and sailing from Portsmouth is presented by Lt Falk who today will be in charge of the ship as she sails. Normally this would be the responsibility of the ship's Navigating Officer, but on this occasion he is taking advantage of the favourable conditions to allow the junior officer to gain some experience — although he still retains overall responsibility for the exercise.

Lt Falk commences with the all-important tidal information. High tide, 4.3m above datum, is at 0944 which will give a minimum of 3.5m below the ship's keel for the initial manoeuvres; 200ft off the berth a tidal stream of only 0.2kt will flow seaward, increasing to 0.8kt at the narrow exit from Portsmouth Harbour (known as the Hole) and 1.2kt off Southsea.

As is normal procedure with aircraft carriers, the ship lies with her starboard side to the jetty in order to give the best view from the offset Bridge during berthing manoeuvres. This has left the ship's head facing northeast and her port side exposed to the light northwesterly breeze. To get the ship moving away from the berth it will be

Above:
The Captain and his officers attend a leaving harbour briefing in one of the air squadron briefing rooms on 2 Deck . . .

Below:
. . . where the Navigating Officer explains how the ship will be manoeuvred from its berth into the main channel.

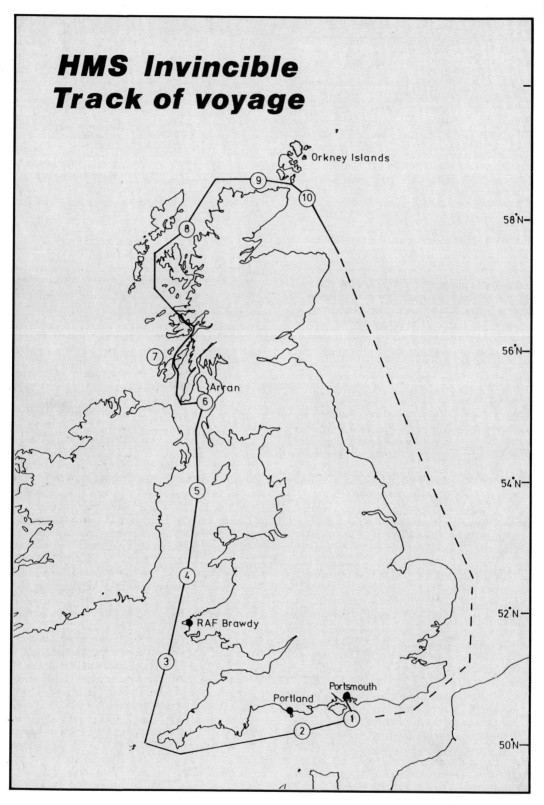

HMS Invincible
Track of voyage

1 THURSDAY 1230 Air Group embarks off the Isle of Wight
2 THURSDAY AFTERNOON Exercises in the English Channel off Portland
3 FRIDAY MORNING Flying Exercises (FLYEX) off the Welsh coast including an Air Defence Exercise (ADEX) involving Hawk aircraft from RAF Brawdy
4 FRIDAY AFTERNOON Full Power machinery trial in the St George's Channel
5 FRIDAY EVENING Night Flying Exercises
6 SATURDAY MORNING Anti-Submarine Exercise (CASEX) in the Firth of Clyde off the Isle of Arran
7 SATURDAY AFTERNOON Pilotage Exercise in the narrow channel between the islands of Islay and Jura
8 SUNDAY MORNING 0730 Start of RAS
9 SUNDAY AFTERNOON 1445 RAS and VERTERP completed
10 SUNDAY EVENING Flying Exercises in the North Sea

necessary to use two tugs. On the bow will be the 450-ton _Bustler_ powered by twin diesels and fitted with Voith Schneider directional propellers, while at the stern will be her sister tug, _Powerful_. In addition, the tug _Forceful_ will be standing by to assist in an emergency or to replace one of the others if required. All these vessels belong to the Royal Maritime Auxiliary Service and will work under the direction of the Admiralty Pilot, Mr Wise, who is embarked aboard _Invincible_. With the ship berthed facing upstream the basic plan is for the tugs to pull the ship sideways away from the jetty for a distance of one cable (200yd), and then to tow the ship astern out into the main channel before using the tug on the bow line to pull the bow round to face downstream. As the ship then gathers way, the tugs will slip and escort _Invincible_ down the main channel until clear of the harbour mouth.

At this point in the briefing the Captain queries the possible use of astern power to assist the tugs. _Invincible_ has relatively small rudders assisted by separate trim tabs — a system which endows the ship with excellent manoeuvrability under normal circumstances — but the Captain wishes to gauge their effectiveness while going astern at slow speeds. Consequently it is decided that at least one shaft will be set at 'Slow Astern' during the initial movement away from the berth.

Throughout the briefing the Captain will interject comment and questions designed not only to clarify matters in his own mind, but also to ensure that all present have fully understood the subject under discussion.

That part of the briefing concerned with leaving Portsmouth is wound up by a list of other shipping movements which will be occurring during the relevant timescale. Thus it is noted that the ocean-going tug _Rollicker_ will be sailing

at 1000 while the Type 22 frigate HMS _Campbeltown_ will be following _Invincible_ at 1100. Prior to the passage of the aircraft carrier, the main channel through the Hole will be closed to traffic between 1010 and 1020. The importance of keeping strictly to the planned schedule is readily apparent.

With the details of the impending departure agreed, discussion turns to the rest of the day's programme for the ship, details of which are briefed by the Navigating Officer. Once clear of the harbour, course will be set past Spithead to a point off the Isle of Wight where the ship's air group will be embarked. The English Channel has many areas which can be set aside for warships to practice their evolutions and today areas Quebec and Zulu are reserved for _Invincible's_ flying operations. The datum point has been set at eight miles, bearing 210° from the Nab Tower and the ship will be in this position at 1230 ready to receive the first wave of four SHARs (Sea Harriers) from 800 Naval Air Squadron (NAS) at that time followed by the remaining four at 1245. The helicopters of 814 and 849 NAS will follow in two waves at 1300 and 1300, although aircraft unserviceabilities have reduced the total to six SKJs (Sea King ASW) and one SKW (Sea King AEW) as against the normal complement of nine and three respectively. Finally, a single shore-based Sea King HC4 will land on at 1400 to drop off 20 squadron personnel before returning to RNAS Yeovilton in Somerset.

On completion of this flying activity the ship will set course to the west for a series of exercises off Portland. These will include an Electronic Warfare jamming demonstration from a FRADU Falcon aircraft, air defence exercises using a towed Rushton target and an intelligence-gathering exercise with HMS _London_, a Type 22 frigate. As if these activities are not enough, the evening will be taken up by a RAS exercise with RFA _Gold Rover_ to test the heavy jackstay equipment prior to refuelling from the same ship.

After a few questions from the Captain the briefing session is virtually complete. One final point decided is the Rig of the Day for leaving harbour. The Royal Navy takes great pride in its ships and men presenting a smart and seaman-like appearance at all times, particularly when operating in full view of other ships and senior officers. On this occasion the ship will adopt Procedure Charlie for leaving harbour which means that only those crew members whose tasks require them to be on deck will be visible, in contrast to the more formal Procedure Alpha where the crew will line the decks for a ceremonial departure or arrival. However, even Procedure Charlie demands that those visible on deck are all wearing the same rig and today it is ordained that this will be Foul Weather Gear (working uniform with heavy-duty waterproof jacket worn over). Traditionally, the port admiral and commanders of other ships will take great enjoyment from being able to signal that they have spotted one crew member not in the Rig of the Day, so it is important for the pride of the ship and her commanding officer that there should be no exceptions today or any other day.

The briefing is completed just after 1000 and all concerned now go to their stations to prepare for sailing. Already the pipe 'Special Sea Duty Men Close Up. Assume Condition Three Yankee' has been broadcast and parties of seamen are mustering on the forecastle and quarterdeck, ready to handle the mooring lines. The term 'Condition Three Yankee' relates to the pre-cautions to be taken for the safety of the ship in terms of watertight integrity and precautions against Nuclear, Biological or Chemical attack (NBCD). The number relates to the state of the ship where 1 is Action Stations, 2 is Defence Stations and 3 is Cruising Stations. The letter 'X' (X-Ray) indicates the normal condition where most watertight doors are open or unlatched and free movement around the ship is possible. 'Y' (Yankee) involves the closure of some doors, particularly those below the waterline and is applied during a RAS, entering or leaving harbour, pilotage in restricted waters and OOW manoeuvres. Condition 'Z' (Zulu) gives full watertight integrity.

As these preparations are in progress, members of the Bridge team make their way forward from the briefing room to the lobby at 2H from where sets of stairs lead up through five deck levels to the Bridge.

Although the Bridge is large by warship standards, there is barely room to move as sailing time approaches. The normal Bridge crew of the Officer of the Watch (OOW) and his second, two Quartermasters, a Signal Yeoman and a Bosun's Mate, is swollen by the extra personnel asociated with the leaving-harbour routine. Each of the four Bridge compass repeaters is manned by a young officer as part of the Fixing team who will constantly take bearings on designated points so that the ship's position can be continuously and very accurately plotted by a fifth officer. On the communications side the Chief Yeoman is on the Bridge and has extra ratings standing by for visual (flag and lamp) and radio signalling. Ready to start the proceedings are the Navigating Officer and his understudy (who we will conveniently designate as N2), the OOW and the ship's Executive Officer while in addition there is the Chief Admiralty Pilot who, on this occasion, is accompanied by another pilot under training. Any spare space is taken up by some of the ship's

senior officers whose job or rank entitles them to a grandstand view of the proceedings. Finally, of course, the Captain is present to ensure that this assembly of experts safely and efficiently carries out its duties.

Although technically complicated, the depar-ture of the ship is a routine procedure and the atmosphere is relaxed. Already the MEOOW (Marine Engineering Officer of the Watch) in the SCC (Ship Control Centre) situated in the bowels of the ship, has reported that all four Olympus gas turbines have been started and are running normally, available for coupling to the two propeller shafts as required. While the ship can — and often does — run on only two engines, it is standard practice to have all four coupled in situations where the sudden loss of a powerplant could be critical. At 1015 a telephone call from aft requests permission from the OOW to land the after gangplank and, following a nod of approval from the Captain, this is given. A few minutes later, at 1022, a confirmatory report, 'After Brow Gone', is received.

By this time the crowd on the Bridge has thinned out as the executive team (Captain, Navigating Officer, N2 and Pilot) have moved to the open Signal Bridge situated immediately above at 05 Deck Level. Except for climbing the masts, this is as high as it is possible to go on the ship and from here an unobstructed view all round the ship is available. At the forward edge is a sheltered compass perlorus with repeaters of some of the Bridge instrumentation and also some communications facilities. Lt Falk plugs in a microphone attached to a long flexible lead which will allow him to pass orders to the Quartermaster (QM) at the helm. Several loud-speakers positioned around the Signal Bridge allow the responses to be heard.

Above:

The tug _Bustler_ edges under _Invincible's_ port bow ready to pick up the towline lowered from the forecastle.

Attention is now focused on the starboard wing of the Signal Bridge from where the jetty and mooring lines can be clearly seen. The Pilot, who is in radio communication with the tugs, checks that they are in position and ready to move. With confirmation received, the N2 issues his first order under the eagle eye of the Navigating Officer:

N2   'Let go fore and aft.'

It is 1023. On the forecastle and quarterdeck the teams of seamen start hauling in the lines as they are released from the quayside bollards by the dockyard workers. As soon as the confirmation, 'All clear fore and aft' is received and repeated from the Bridge, the Pilot relays this information to the tugs which then commence to pull the ship away from the jetty. At the same time the OOW speaks into his microphone.

OOW   'Slow Ahead port.'

Almost immediately this instruction is repeated by the Quartermaster at the wheel on the Bridge. Another instruction follows:

OOW   'Starboard thirty-five.'

Above:
Last link with the shore, the after brow is lifted away by crane a few minutes before sailing.

Below:
'Let Go Forrard!' Dockyard workers prepare to release the bowline on instructions radioed from the ship.

Above:
The actions of the tugs are co-ordinated by the Admiralty Pilot who communicates using a hand-held VHF set.

Left:
Under the influence of the tugs, *Invincible* moves slowly away from the jetty.

Again, this instruction is repeated and after a distinct pause comes a further response:

QM   'Thirty-five of starboard wheel on, Sir.'

Another order blares from the speaker.

OOW   'Slow Astern starboard.'
QM   'Slow Astern starboard . . . starboard tele-graph repeats Slow Astern, Sir.'

By now the ship is just beginning to move, the helm and telegraph orders designed to swing the stern of the ship away from the jetty, aiding the tugs as they ease the ship out into the tidal stream and attempt to swing the stern around to port. As the ship clears the jetty, power is increased on the starboard shaft.

OOW   'Half Astern starboard.'

Above:
'Slow Astern Starboard'. Lt Falk passes helm and telegraph to the Quartermaster on the Bridge below by means of a microphone on a flying lead.

Below:
The Quartermaster acknowledges a helm order through his boom microphone and alters course using the aircraft-style control wheel.

With port shaft running ahead and the starboard shaft astern a turning movement of the stern to port is established, aiding the rudders which are fully angled to starboard. Already *Invincible* is at least one cable off the jetty and the stern is slowly coming round to the required direction. However, care must be taken not to allow the ship to come too close to the ships moored by the North Corner

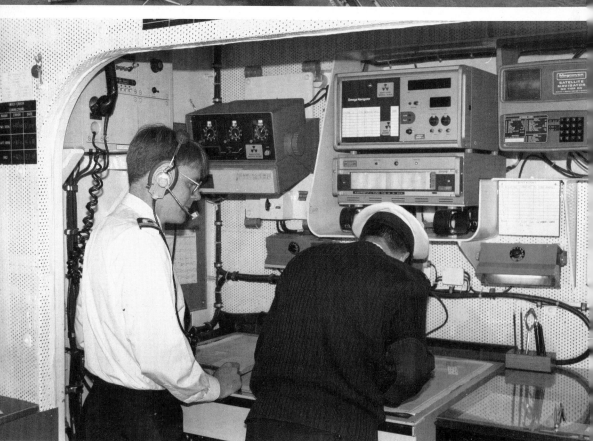

Jetty now lying under the starboard quarter, so
the OOW reduces astern power now that the ship
is moving.

OOW 'Slow Astern starboard.'
QM 'Slow Astern starboard.'
The seaman assisting the Quartermaster turns
the knob on the small telegraph, moving the
pointer to 'Slow Astern'. Immediately the outer
pointer moves to 'Slow Astern' accompanied by a
momentary high-pitched bell-ring which indicates that the order has been acknowledged from
the SCC.

QM 'Starboard telegraph repeats Slow Astern.'

The Quartermaster calls into his boom-mounted
microphone so that the report is heard on the
Signal Bridge above.

By now the two tugs have *Invincible* well in
hand with *Powerful* providing the main pull on
the stern while *Bustler* steadies the bow. The N2
calls for the port shaft to be stopped and then set
at 'Slow Astern' now that the ship's stern is
facing out towards the main channel, and shortly
afterwards gives only his second helm order:

N2 'Midships!'

This is repeated by the Quartermaster who
watches the rudder angle indicator as he turns
the small control wheel until it indicates zero
deflection.

QM 'Wheel amidships.'

While the N2 and the Pilot have been engaged in
moving the ship from the jetty, other members of
the Bridge team have been busy. The Radio
Operator manning the communications console
on the starboard side of the Bridge has reported
to Portsmouth Port Operations that the ship has
left her berth. At each of the four Bridge compass
repeaters, officers of the Fixing team are taking
bearings from prominent features and navigation
marks. As each bearing is called out it is noted
down by the Second OOW who is in charge of the
Fixing team and plotted on the chart by another

officer. In this way the ship's position can be plotted to within a few metres and continuously updated.

The chart in use at this stage is a large scale (1:7500) one showing Portsmouth Harbour, No 2631 in the complete range of Admiralty charts covering the whole of the British Isles. As an illustration of the amount of detail possible at this scale, HMS *Invincible* – if drawn on the chart – would be almost exactly 1in long!

At this stage the ship has cleared the North Corner Jetty and is approaching the middle of the main channel which, at this point, is regularly dredged to maintain a minimum depth of 8.5m. As it is just after high water the depth meter, repeating from the Type 778 Depth Finder, shows a steady depth of 14m. The Fixing team confirm to the N2 that he is almost at the point where the next manoeuvre must begin – stopping the ship and commencing a turn through almost 90° in order to face down the main channel to the harbour exit. He, in turn, is able to confirm this from his own observations and calls down for both shafts to be set to 'Stop'. The Pilot instructs *Powerful* to ease off her pull astern and directs *Bustler* to move around to the starboard side of the bow from where she can start assisting the turn on to a southerly course. At this point *Bustler's* Voith Schneider ducted directional

Above:
Once in the centre of the channel, clear of the jetties, the tug *Bustler* pulls *Invincible's* bows around to starboard in order to face downstream. In the background is the RFA *Blue Rover.*

Above right:
Almost round! The ship is now nearly facing the harbour entrance, visible off the starboard bow.

Right:
The Queen's Harbourmaster follows *Invincible* in his launch in order to check that the departure goes smoothly and to be on hand if there are any problems.

propellers come into play as the tug swings itself sideways through an arc, whose radius is defined by the line joining her to *Invincible's* bow, until she ends up pulling at almost a right angle to the line of the larger ship. A new litany of orders and responses now follows:

N2 'Slow Astern starboard.'
QM 'Slow Astern starboard.'
N2 'Slow Ahead port.'
QM 'Slow Ahead port.'
N2 'Starboard thirty-five.'
QM 'Starboard thirty-five . . . thirty-five degrees of starboard wheel on!'

Under the combination of the thrust of the engines, the rudder angle and the pull of the tug, *Invincible's* bow is slowly forced round to starboard. As the swing develops, the starboard shaft is stopped and then brought momentarily to 'Half Ahead', giving the ship some forward momentum so that the rudder can begin to act.

With the ship safely clear of the jetties and turning on to course in the main channel, there is no further need for the services of the stern tug, *Powerful*. Both shafts are brought to 'Stop' in case the towline should foul the screws when released and Lt Falk's voice booms out over the Bridge speaker, repeated on the bow and quarterdeck, as he gives his unambiguous orders:

Left:
The Navigating Officer and Captain discuss the situation as the tugs turn the ship in mid-channel.

Below left:
Her work completed, the tug *Powerful* releases the stern line and moves clear of the ship. In the background are various ships laid up in Fareham Creek.

Below:
With the tugs cast off, *Invincible* proceeds down channel under her own power. Visible to port are the Royal Yacht *Britannia*, the masts of HMS *Warrior* and the distinctive shape of the Semaphore Tower from where the port's operations are controlled.

'Do NOT slip *Powerful* go, STANDBY to slip *Powerful*.'
A short pause to allow the order to be understood.

N2 'Let go *Powerful!*'

As *Invincible* releases the line it is quickly hauled in by the tug and the quarterdeck officer calls the Bridge to confirm that it is clear of the water. *Bustler* hovers near the stern in case she should still be needed, but for all practical purposes her work is done. More orders:

OOW 'Slow Ahead starboard.'
QM 'Slow Ahead starboard . . . thirty-five degrees of starboard wheel still on.'

The latter is a routine reminder of the rudder setting as the ship continues to swing round. The N2 now gives his first course direction to the Quartermaster at the wheel:

N2 'Altering one seven three degrees.'

The Quartermaster glances at the compass strip in front of him and responds:

QM 'Passing one five three degrees . . . coming to heading one seven three.'

It is now 1035, only 12min since the mooring lines were cast off from the jetty. *Invincible* is now

almost facing down the main channel as the Fixing team confirm that she is only 20m right of the intended course for moving down the upper reaches of Portsmouth Harbour.

OOW 'Midships.'

As the ship's head comes round towards the required course of 173°, the N2 centres the rudder and checks the bearing of the Fort Blockhouse Lookout Tower just off the starboard bow. This will be his 'head marker' for the initial run down the harbour. In the meantime the work of the tugs is virtually completed as the ship gathers steerage way and the Pilot calls down:

Left:
The tug *Bustler*, still accompanying *Invincible*, passes the restored Victorian battleship HMS *Warrior*.

Below:
Approaching the 'Hole'. The narrowness of the entrance to Portsmouth Harbour can be appreciated in this view from *Invincible's* Signal Platform.

Below right:
Leaving Portsmouth, the Spit Sand Fort is visible directly ahead and provides an excellent navigation marker.

Pilot 'Standby to slip *Bustler*.'

The ship's head is still swinging and a touch of opposite rudder is required to check it.

OOW 'Port thirty-five.'
QM 'Port thirty-five . . . passing one six three.'

As the compass swings round to 173° the rudder is centred again and the order is given to release the tug.

Pilot 'Slip *Bustler*.'

A few seconds pass.
Forecastle Officer '*Bustler* gone!'

The buff and black tug can be seen from the Bridge as she edges away from under the bow and takes station on *Invincible's* port side. With a clear channel ahead and free of the tugs the ship is free to proceed.

OOW 'Steer one seven three degrees.'
QM 'Half Ahead both engines, revolutions six zero.'

The telegraph operator rings down for 'Half Ahead' and sets the rpm tallies below the telegraph indicators to read 60. *Invincible* is now beginning to move down the harbour towards the open sea, passing the moored warships at the Naval Base on the port side and the outline of Burrow Island with the buildings of the Royal Clarence Victualling Yard behind to starboard. A small flotilla including the two tugs, a police launch, the Queen's Harbourmaster's launch and a police boat take station like a bunch of courtiers following a queen on her stately progress.

As the ship settles on course it is no longer necessary to con the ship from the open Signal Bridge and so the Captain briefly takes over the handling of the ship while the N2, accompanied by the Navigating Officer, makes his way down to the Compass Platform on the Main Bridge. Once in position he reports to the Captain.

Navigating Officer 'I am on the Bridge, Sir, ready to take the ship.'

The Captain responds immediately.

Captain 'Roger. One seven three degrees ordered, just coming on to course now. Half Ahead, revolutions six zero. You have the ship!'

Navigating Officer 'I have the ship, Sir'.

At the same time he receives a confirmatory report from the Quartermaster that the ship is steady on course 174°.

The Captain, Navigator and Pilot now also leave the Signal Bridge, leaving only a couple of signallers and the Side Party ready to exchange courtesies, as required, with other ships and the Port Admiral. Once below, the Captain installs himself in the raised chair at his command console on the port side of the Bridge from where he can monitor the actions of the Bridge team. The N2 checks the bearing on his head marker and orders a small alteration of course to 176° while the second OOW reports that the depth of water is remaining constant at 15m, further confirmation that the ship is correctly positioned in the main channel.

Now that the ship is underway the radar operators in the Operations Room below are checking and identifying various contacts on their screens so that this information can be fed into the ship's ADAWS computer system. In this way they can also advise the OOW of any ships which might present a potential hazard to *Invincible*. One of the operators manning the main Plot has direct contact with the Bridge by means of an open intercom line relayed to a loudspeaker on the Bridge. Already Plot has warned the Bridge of a large contact moving across the main channel from starboard to port ahead of the ship. This has been identified as one of the commercial ferries pulling in to Clarence Pier on the east side of the main channel, leading out from the Hole. Now comes another call.

Plot 'Bridge, Plot. There is a small contact by Number Four Buoy heading up the channel which will pass close to starboard.'

The OOW checks in the indicated area with his binoculars and is able to report that the contact is a small launch keeping to the small boat channel which leads close inshore on the west side of the harbour entrance. This is relayed to the Plot and added to the file of target information held by the computer.

The time is now 1039 and after checking the ship's position, maintained on the chart by the OOW and his Fixing team, the N2 calculates that the ship has one-and-a-half cables to run to the first change of course and he reports this fact to the Captain.

N2 'One-and-a-half cables to wheel over, Sir.'
Captain 'Very good, carry on when ready.'

However, before turning, a small complication arises. The Harbourmaster (QHM) has called on the VHF channel to report that a working party on a pontoon alongside one of the piles off Victoria Pier, just past the Hole, have requested that *Invincible* should slow down when passing in

order to avoid damage from her wash. Already Lt Falk has obtained the Captain's approval to go to 12kt once clear of the harbour but, after a brief discussion, it is agreed to reduce this until past the pontoon although the ship must maintain around 6kt in order to ensure adequate steerage in the restricted waters of the harbour mouth. The Navigating Officer, monitoring all these proceedings, takes the radio to confirm to the QHM that the ship will slow down.

At 1040 the wheel-over position is reached and orders are given to alter course to 164° as *Invincible* passes abeam the Portsmouth Harbour railway station. This new course will be held for three cables (600yd) and will take the ship to the narrow harbour mouth where a further alteration to port will bring the ship on to a course of 154° for the run through the Hole. With everything running to plan there is a lull in the steady stream of orders, intercom communications and radio calls, allowing the N2 to appraise the Captain of the ship's progress and details of his intentions for taking the ship through the Hole. This is acknowledged with a curt 'Roger', as is a report from the Fixing team that the ship is exactly on course.

At 6kt the ship takes 3min to cover the three cables to the new wheel over point and the time is 1043 as orders are given to alter course to 154°. A certain tension is now apparent as the ship enters the narrow harbour mouth. The deep water channel is only 100yd wide here — giving little room for manoeuvre in the event of an emergency. However, there are no problems as *Invincible* steers majestically down the channel, affording a stirring sight to a small crowd which has gathered on the ramparts of the Round Tower on the eastern side of the Hole.

As the ship has passed down the harbour the party on the Signal Bridge has been kept busy ensuring that the necessary naval courtesies have been paid. On the port side the flag of the C-in-C Naval Home Command flying aboard HMS *Victory* has been saluted while to starboard the flag at HMS *Dolphin*, the submarine base, is also saluted. In each case the Side Party pipes 'Still' on their boatswain's pipes and all on deck stand to attention and face in the direction called. A return call of the 'Still' followed by 'Carry On' is piped from ashore, at which point the ship's party pipes 'Carry On' and the exchange is completed. Thus the simple niceties of naval tradition are maintained.

As *Invincible* heads through the harbour mouth into the more open waters of the Solent the tugs, which are trailing astern in case they should still be needed, are stood down. A radio call on the VHF by the Navigating Officer thanks them for their services as they turn and head back to their

Above:
There is always a good crowd on the Round Tower to watch a warship sail. When *Invincible* sailed for the Falklands in 1982 these buildings and walls were covered in people giving the Task Force a rousing send-off.

Right:
A hovercraft from Southsea to the Isle of Wight passes ahead of *Invincible* as the ship passes out of the Hole.

berths in the Naval Base. Ahead of the ship, the Plot warns the Bridge of a hovercraft pulling out of the Terminal by Clarence Pier on the port side. It is clearly visible as it crosses two cables ahead and moves away at high speed to starboard.

Already the Bridge team has unconsciously moved into the routine of looking ahead to the next wheel over point, checking position with the Fixing team and anticipating the turn with a few degrees of rudder before the actual point is reached. Although the waters are opening out at this point, the deep channel is still relatively narrow and precise navigation is vital. The Fixing team confirm that the ship is still on course as the next turning point, two cables west of Clarence Pier, is reached at 1044.

N2 'Port ten, steer one four eight.'

The N2 starts to bring the ship round, making two small turns rather than one large alteration in order to follow the line of the channel. As the Quartermaster reports steady on 148°, further rudder is applied and orders given to increase speed to 12kt now that the ship is well clear of the harbour mouth.

N2 'Port fifteen, altering one four zero . . . revolutions seven right, steer one four zero.'

As these orders are passed, one of the Fixing team can be heard calling out the change in bearing of the light on Fort Blockhouse away on the starboard quarter.

Fixing Team 'Light bearing three two three . . . bearing three two four . . .'

QM 'Seven eight revolutions passed and repeated, Sir.'

The telegraphs ring as the instructions for 78 revolutions is acknowledged and the ship perceptively picks up speed and settles on to the new course of 140°. This will be held for almost exactly 10 cables (1 nautical mile) to a point three-and-a-half cables south of Southsea Castle when the ship will bear 068° from the Spit Sand Fort in the Solent. The latter is one of a series of forts built in the Solent during the mid-19th century to defend the naval anchorages and harbour in the event of a French attack. However, the need for them evaporated almost at the time they were completed and consequently they are often referred to as 'Palmerston's Follies' after the Prime Minister of the time. They remain today as useful markers for navigation, having been built to last by the Victorian engineers.

The run down towards the green buoy off Southsea Castle, which marks the turn in the channel, is straightforward and is only interrupted by several calls from the Plot to advise of various contacts which will pass close to *Invincible*. All of these are easily seen and identified from the Bridge as the visibility is virtually unlimited. Lt Falk consults with the Captain and Navigating Officer over the next stages of the passage while, at the same time, keeping a close eye on the fixes being continuously plotted on the chart. His head marker on this course is the Nab Tower, another of the forts, some nine miles ahead.

At two cables to run to the wheel over, the N2 advises the Captain of his intention to start the turn slightly early at one cable. The new course will be 180° and by the time that the ship has swung through 40° it should have run on to neatly intercept the required track. With the Captain's

Top:
The Bridge team have now left the Signal Platform and the ship is being navigated normally from the Compass Platform. The Captain has taken his chair on the port side from where he can continue to monitor the operation.

Above:
The Spit Sand Fort, one of many built in Victorian times to defend Portsmouth, is left to starboard.

approval he orders 10° of starboard rudder, shortly increasing this to 20°. The ship begins to swing to starboard, perhaps a little quicker than anticipated so that it is necessary to ease the rudder angle and eventually to order opposite rudder to straighten up on 180°.

N2 'Ease to ten.'
QM 'Ten degrees of starboard wheel on, Sir.'
N2 'Midships.'
QM 'Wheel amidships.'
N2 'Port ten.'
QM 'Ten of port on, passing one six zero degrees.'
N2 'Midships, steer one eight zero.'

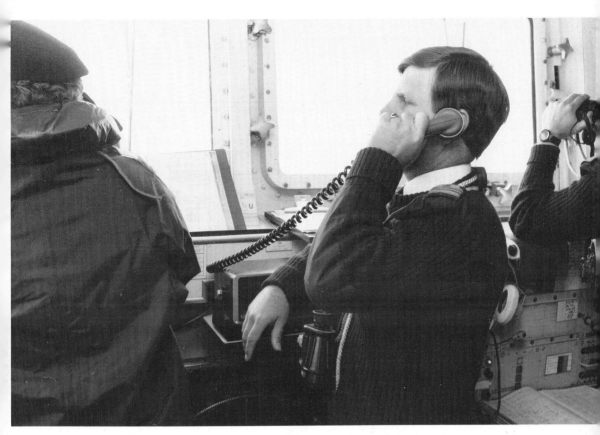

As the ship settles on to course, the N2 takes a quick bearing on the Spit Sand Fort to starboard and checks the resulting 250° against the marks on his sailing plan which he has been constantly using to check progress. The time is 1051, nearly half-an-hour since slipping from the jetty, and the most difficult parts of the departure from Portsmouth now have been completed. The next turn is due in 1.3nm as the ship is about to pass between No Man's Land and Horse Sand forts where an alteration to 130° will be made. After a run of 1.9nm a further turn to port will bring the ship round to 107° and a 3nm run before the final turn on to 180° takes the ship out of the marked channels and towards the deeper waters to the east of the Isle of Wight.

Above:
The Navigating Officer uses the VHF radio on the starboard side of the Bridge to talk to the Master of the *Esso Tees* as the two ships approach.

After safely completing the turn abeam Horse Sand Fort at 1058, the situation is complicated by the presence of two large ships approaching from the southeast, both having been picked up on radar some time previously and their proximity predicted. The first ship is a P&O ferry with its distinctive kingfisher blue hull and white upper-works. A radio call on the VHF confirms that she

Below:
Viewed from *Invincible's* Bridge, the *Esso Tees* passes away to starboard.

Above:
The N2 takes a bearing on the Nab Tower using one of the compass repeaters on the Bridge.

is inbound to Portsmouth and as she is correctly positioned on the east side of the main channel presents no hazard to *Invincible*. The ferry subsequently passes safely by on the port side but the second vessel, the large coastal tanker *Esso Tees*, presents a more difficult problem. The tanker is entering the Solent from the southeast and proceeding up the channel to the Fawley refinery in Southampton Water and on present course will pass just ahead of *Invincible* at the point at which the next turn on to 107° is due. The Navigating Officer calls the tanker on VHF explaining *Invincible's* intended actions and asking if the *Esso Tees* can alter course to starboard in compliance with the normal maritime rules. However the Master declines to do this, presumably because he is heavily laden and a turn to starboard would put him towards the shallows on the north side of the channel. Instead he suggests that *Invincible* make her turn early and pass down his starboard side. The Navigating Officer agrees to this and the radio conversation is terminated on an amicable note.

With the Captain's approval the helm orders are given and the aircraft carrier swings to port leaving the tanker to pass to starboard. However, this turn puts the ship a little to the north of the intended track so, once the *Esso Tees* has passed by, course is altered to 112° for a couple of minutes until the ship regains the planned course and steadies up again on 107°. At this point the depth is reported as 29m and the main channel is marked by the green Dean Elbow and Dean Tail buoys to port, and the Nab East and Nab End Red buoys to starboard.

The flotilla of tugs and small craft which have been accompanying *Invincible* has gradually fallen away leaving only the black and white pilot cutter running close alongside. With the ship now well clear of the harbour approaches and coming to the end of the marked channels, the Pilot is no longer needed and after being thanked by the Captain for his assistance, he makes his way down to the open waist of the ship on 4 Deck where the companionway has been rigged. Although the ship is making 15kt by now, the sea is absolutely calm and there is no problem in stepping on to the pilot cutter as it comes close alongside, under the overhanging mass of *Invincible*. As soon as the Pilot is safely on board, the cutter sheers away to starboard and heads at full speed back to Portsmouth while the companionway is swung inboard and stowed.

Aboard *Invincible* the last few rituals of leaving harbour are being completed. The Fixing Team on the Bridge is stood down and at 1118 a pipe is made over the ship's broadcast system.

'Fall Out Special Sea Duty Men. Assume Condition Three X-Ray.'

The party of seamen and signallers on the Signal Bridge, as well as the various deck parties, can now stand down while the routine of the ship is left to the duty watch. The Bridge has now emptied of all but the normal watchkeeping team and a few of the ship's senior officers in discussion with the Captain. However, the ship is not quite clear of the harbour approaches and at 1122 a turn on to 180° is executed, setting course to pass eight cables to the east of the Nab Tower — the last of the forts. By passing to the east, the ship is kept clear of the buoyed and dredged channel which is set aside for use by deep draught vessels (such as the supertankers running to Fawley) and which passes to the west of the Nab.

While the ship runs south the Captain and Navigator hold a short debriefing session with the N2 on a couple of problems thrown up during the departure from Portsmouth. It is noted that some difficulty was experienced in steering the ship when going astern from the jetty and the use of tugs in such situations would obviously be essential. The Navigator makes a few comments on the N2's handling of the ship and offers some advice for future occasions but, on the whole, the morning's programme has gone well.

At 1130, precisely on schedule, *Invincible* passes abeam the Nab Tower. Now that the ship is well out to sea the Captain instructs the OOW to take the ship to the designated rendezvous (RV) for embarking her aircraft and then, with a quick glance around to check that all is in order, goes below to his sea cabin. The RV is 8nm on a bearing of 210° from the Nab Tower and the ship is to be in that position at 1230, 1hr ahead. Accordingly the OOW orders the ship on to a southwesterly course and reduces speed to 8kt.

When the Sea Harrier jets and Sea King helicopters arrive overhead the Bridge will again be the scene of much activity but, for the moment, it is relatively quiet. On the flightdeck the aircraft handlers can be seen checking their vehicles and equipment in preparation for the arrival of the first aircraft, while those off-duty below decks are taking an early lunch. It is perhaps a good time now to have a closer look at the Bridge, its layout and equipment, and the routines of those who run the ship.

Right:
With *Invincible* safely clear of the approaches to Portsmouth, the pilot launch comes under the ship's starboard side and prepares to pick up the Pilot.

Below:
Once the ship is safely at sea the aircraft handlers begin to prepare the flightdeck for the arrival of the Air Group in the afternoon, while on the Bridge above a normal routine is established.

ON THE BRIDGE

HMS *Invincible's* enclosed Bridge, high up at the forward end of the island superstructure, is the focal point for the navigation and conduct of the ship. By warship standards it is spacious and being over 80ft above the water line offers an excellent view around the ship. In fact this part of the ship, commonly referred to as the Bridge, is properly termed the Compass Platform and must be regarded as one of two nerve centres in the ship. While the routine running of the ship centres on the Bridge, the conduct of naval warfare operations is run from the ship's Operations Room on one of the lower decks. The interaction of these two centres is unique to

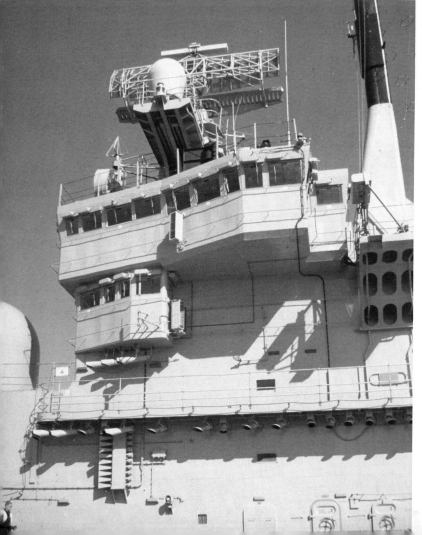

Left:
Invincible's **Bridge, or Compass Platform as it should correctly be termed, is four decks above the flightdeck. At its after end is the projecting Flyco cabin while an Admiral's small Flag Bridge is situated immediately below. The mast above the Bridge structure carries the long range Type 1022 radar and satellite communications equipment.**

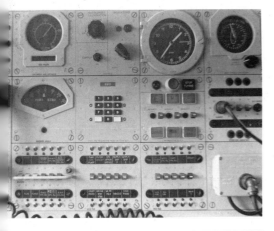

Top:

The Captain's console on the port side of the Bridge. The two rows of three rectangular buttons beneath the clock are used in liaison with Flyco to give permission for various flying operations.

Above:

This CRT gives a readout from the ship's ADAWS computer system and allows the OOW to see information relating to ship targets which may pass within a preselected distance. Looking at this display it can be seen that Track No 2620, presently bearing 215° at 5.8nm from *Invincible*, is proceeding on a course of 353° at a speed of 7kt and at its closest point will pass 3.2 miles away on a bearing of 160°.

warships and produces additional workload and stress on the Bridge team which is not normally associated with mercantile operations.

Anyone familiar with the Bridge of a modern Royal Navy frigate or destroyer would be at home at once aboard *Invincible*. The degree of standardisation in layout and equipment aboard RN ships is immediately apparent as one steps on to the Compass Platform via a door on the starboard side of the rear bulkhead. This is only done, of course, after the traditional request for access: 'Officer of the Watch, permission to come on the Bridge, Sir!'

Along the forward face of the Bridge are the various panels containing instrumentation, telephone and intercom controls, and the Quartermaster's wheel and engine controls. The left-hand panel is the Captain's console which has a clock and instruments showing ship's speed, rudder angle and the relative wind over the deck. In addition he has a row of telephone and intercom keyboards together with a clip-on handset. One important display consists of two rows of three backlit buttons, the top red and the lower green, which are used to give or cancel permission for various flying operations on the flightdeck. When present on the Bridge, the Captain sits at his console on a raised high-back chair from where he commands a good view of the flightdeck to port, as well as being able to survey the situation ahead of the ship.

To the right of the Captain's console is a CRT display showing a readout from the ship's ADAWS computer. This uses radar-extracted data to calculate the closest point to which other vessels will come in relation to *Invincible*. In the Operations Room each new radar contact is given a four-figure track number and the information on the target's course, speed and CPA then appears on the Bridge display once the other vessel is within a preset distance. Thus, for example, the display could be programmed to show data on all vessels within 15 miles whose CPA is within five miles, allowing the OOW adequate time to take avoiding action if necessary.

Next to the ADAWS readout is a small console housing a Plessey Type 1006 navigation radar display. *Invincible* is equipped with two of these high-resolution radars which, on the Bridge, are used mainly for observing the relative position of other ships during poor visibility and to determine the range and bearing of ships, buoys, lighthouses, coastlines, and other prominent features. The Type 1006, manufactured by Kelvin Hughes, is an I-Band radar widely used throughout the fleet, although later ships have the more modern Type 1007 with much enhanced raster scan displays.

The PPI display on *Invincible's* Bridge can be set to show ranges from as close as half-a-mile out to a maximum of 96 miles, although detection of surface targets will be limited to the radar horizon. Turning the bearing marker control allows a bearing line on the screen to be laid on to a target, while rotating the range cursor generates a variable range ring which again can be made to intersect the target. The exact range is then read off an LED readout above the screen.

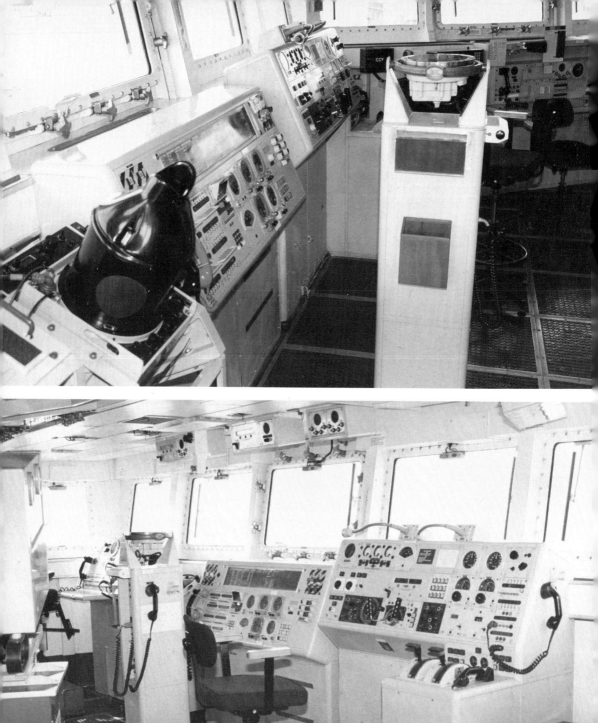

Left:
Looking to starboard from the Captain's seat. On the left is the shaded screen of the Type 1006 navigation radar and beyond that is the central console used by the OOW.

Below left:
A general view of the Bridge looking to port. In the centre is the OOW's console and compass pelorus, and on the right is the Quartermaster's console.

The centre console at the front of the Bridge is used by the OOW and displays the full range of data required to efficiently handle the ship. A panel of intercom and telephone keyboards is set on the left-hand side while in the centre are readouts of rudder angle, ship's log (speed), and depth under the keel. At the top corners of the console are clearly marked and caged buttons which release marker buoys and lifebelts in the event of a man overboard. Between these buttons is an illuminated panel of which the OOW notes information to show the status of various items of the ship's equipment. Thus he can note which radars and sonars are operating, which engines are running or shut down, whether various weapon mountings are live or safe and the state of the various navigation aids. A set of dials shows the bearing and elevation of the various high-powered satellite communications aerials. Knowledge of these settings is important as their transmissions are dangerous and they can also interact with the electronics of weapon systems and aircraft.

Immediately behind the OOW's console, in the centre of the Bridge, is the compass pelorus. Apart from the standard gyro compass repeater

The Bridge Team

CAPTAIN   The ship's Commanding Officer with overall responsibility for the efficient running of the ship and the discharge of any tasks or duties assigned to the ship. Although often present on the Bridge, he may also oversee the Conduct of the ship from the Command position in the Operations Room below decks.

EXECUTIVE OFFICER   The Commander. Responsible to the Captain for the efficient routine administration and running of the ship and her crew. He is one of three officers who is authorised to take Conduct of the ship (see text).

NAVIGATING OFFICER   Also known as the Navigator or Pilot, a Lt-Cdr by rank. Fully responsible to the Captain for all matters concerning the safe navigation of the ship. Although not a watchkeeping officer, his sea cabin is immediately adjacent to the Bridge so that he is always on hand to assist and give advice to the OOW. Also authorised to have Conduct of the ship.

OFFICER OF THE WATCH   Normally a Lt or Sub-Lt by rank. The officer having charge of the ship during the period of his Watch, he is responsible for the routine safe operation of the ship but will keep the Captain fully advised at all times of any matters affecting the safety of the ship or her aircraft, and may call on the Navigating Officer at any time for advice and assistance.

SECOND OOW   Generally an Officer Under Training (OUT) with the rank of Midshipman or Sub-Lt. His duties involve assisting the OOW with particular reference to the navigation of the ship and keeping an accurate update of the ship's position on the chart.

QUARTERMASTER   A senior rating who steers the ship under the direction of the OOW. He is normally assisted by another seaman who transmits the OOW's engine orders to the SCC by means of telegraphs and revolution counters.

SIGNAL YEOMAN   Communications Branch ratings responsible for exchanges of signals between the ship and other vessels, normally by voice radio but also by W/T, flag, semaphore and light signals. Normal complement on the Bridge is a Leading Radio Operator assisted by another RO.

BOSUN'S MATE   Junior rating responsible for manning the Bridge telephone switchboard and, when directed, making pipes on the ship's internal broadcast system.

LOOKOUTS   Two seamen are stationed on the Bridge to act as additional lookouts at night, and by day when circumstances require them. At normal cruising stations they are not closed up and the OOW is responsible for maintaining a lookout.

mounted on top, the pelorus also incorporates a small communications panel and wooden pockets holding easy reference lists of standard procedures to be used under various circumstances. In fact the compass is one of four repeaters mounted on the Bridge, the others being mounted one on either beam and one right aft in the Flyco cabin. These all can be driven by the Master Mk 23 Gyro Compass or the NCS (Naval Compass Stabiliser) Mk 1 buried deep in the bowels of the ship which is a gyro-stabilised platform providing a heading reference for navigation and three-axis stabilisation data for the various weapon systems. Alternatively the compass can be driven from the Ship's Inertial Navigation System (SINS) which has its own gyro platform.

All four repeaters are fitted with sights to enable bearings to be taken. For course steering purposes there are a number of illuminated strip readouts of the ship's heading and several of these are mounted in overhead consoles where they are visible by the OOW and the Quartermaster.

To right of the OOW's panel is another console containing the controls for steering the ship and operating the engines. Despite the size and bulk of the ship it is steered by a small aircraft-style control wheel operated by the helmsman or Quartermaster who sits at the left-hand side of the console. In front of him is a strip readout from the gyro compass which is his main

reference for course steering. On either side of the wheel are panels for setting up and engaging an autopilot system which will keep the ship on any required course – again similar to aircraft installations. However, this equipment is rarely used aboard *Invincible* except on long passages. To the right of the compass strip is an alarm panel which will indicate the failure of any system vital to the steering of the ship such as compass or gyro failures, SINS or NCS failures and loss of steering motors on either rudder. To the left are switches for the navigation and masthead lights.

One set of dials on the Quartermaster's console betray the fact that this is not a merchant ship. A small panel shows the status and depth of the Type 182 Foxer which is sometimes streamed astern to act as a decoy for homing torpedoes and to contain enemy sonars.

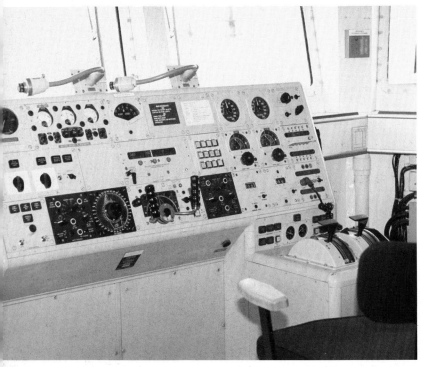

The right-hand half of the console is taken up with the means of communicating with the Ship Control Centre (SCC) and controlling power output to the propeller shafts. Provision is made, by means of two throttle-type levers, for this to be done directly from the Bridge but, in practice, this is almost never done. Instead power requirements are rung using miniature telegraphs and rpm indicators. Both the Quartermaster and the Telegraph Operator use the boom microphones mounted atop the console for acknowledging and repeating orders. A detailed description of the control and operation of the ship's engines is given in a later chapter.

The Quartermaster's console is at the extreme starboard side of the forward edge of the Bridge. To his right, the side of the Bridge angles back sharply to house the radio communications centre normally manned by two operators facing to starboard. The various transmitters and receivers are operated from the Communications Centre below decks, but any required channel or network can be fed into the Bridge console and selected at the push of a button. Normally the Radio Operator will monitor the channel on his headset, but transmissions can be fed through to speakers on the Bridge if required.

A standard commercial multi-channel VHF transceiver is fitted at this side of the Bridge, allowing quick and direct communications with other ships and civil shore radio stations, such as the Coastguard, for normal maritime purposes. This facility is often used to talk to merchant ships when co-ordinating movements to avoid a risk of collision. A second compact VHF set is also being fitted on to the compass pelorus for the direct use of the OOW.

To the left of the Radio Operator is a large board on which the disposition of friendly ships in company, together with their callsigns, can be marked using a chinagraph pencil. This is a handy reference, particularly when using visual signalling techniques which can be either by means of flag hoists from the open Signal Deck immediately aft of the enclosed Bridge, or by lamps on the Signal Bridge above. In these days of sophisticated electronic warfare, when any electromagnetic emission can betray a ship's presence and identity, visual signalling is often used and it is important that the skills involved are constantly practised.

Behind the Radio Operator sits the Bo'sun's Mate manning a telephone console mounted against one of the central Bridge bulkheads. Although all members of the Bridge team have access to their own telephone keyboards, most non-urgent and routine communication with the Bridge is routed through this console. Access to the ship's internal broadcast system is normally made through here – after gaining the permission of the OOW – to make a 'pipe', the most common call being to contact crew members who cannot be located by other means. Thus the ship regularly echoes to pipes such as: 'Leading Seaman Johnson, two zero eight,' the number indicating the internal telephone number for the seaman to call.

The starboard wing of the Bridge, running aft from beside the radio operators, is normally empty apart from the the gyro compass mounted on the side. However, during certain evolutions such as berthing and RAS, the Navigating Officer will move to this side where he has a better view of what is going on. In these circumstances some of the Bridge windows can be removed and a chair mounted on a raised rostrum can be installed.

Against the rear bulkhead of the Bridge, immediately aft of the compass pelorus, is the chart table which acts as a centre for the navigation of the ship at all times. Set back in an alcove, which can be curtained off at night, it is surrounded by an array of modern navigation equipment and stands on lockers and shelves which hold the selection of charts and reference documents for the area in which the ship is operating.

The main navigation aids – all mounted on the bulkhead above the chart table – are Decca, Omega, a satellite navigation system, and the Type 778 Depth Finder, all these being standard equipment in most RN ships. Both Decca and Omega are hyperbolic navigation systems, producing a grid of position lines by comparing the time at which signals are received from various slave transmitter stations with the time at which a master signal is received. Decca is widely used but the transmitting stations are grouped in local 'chains' and consequently it is normally used in coastal and offshore passages where coverage is good. Position fixing is by means of reading off position lines, each consisting of a lane identification (normally a letter and a number) followed by lateral displacement within the lane indicated by a dial below the lane identification. The intersection of two or more position lines obtained in this way shows the ship's position when the grid formed by the Decca lanes is overprinted on the normal charts for easy plotting.

Omega is a worldwide system using a relatively small number of stations transmitting signals at

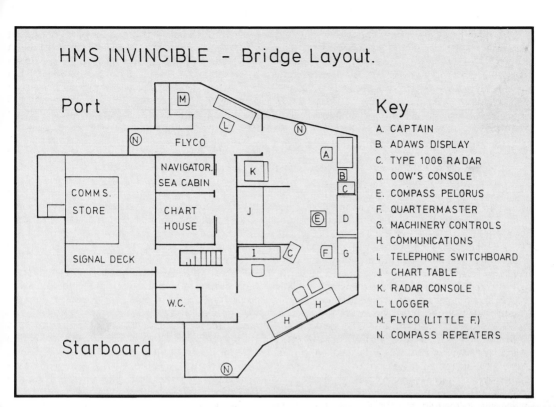

HMS INVINCIBLE – Bridge Layout.

Port

Key

A. CAPTAIN
B. ADAWS DISPLAY
C. TYPE 1006 RADAR
D. OOW'S CONSOLE
E. COMPASS PELORUS
F. QUARTERMASTER
G. MACHINERY CONTROLS
H. COMMUNICATIONS
I. TELEPHONE SWITCHBOARD
J. CHART TABLE
K. RADAR CONSOLE
L. LOGGER
M. FLYCO (LITTLE F.)
N. COMPASS REPEATERS

Labels on layout: M, L, N, FLYCO, NAVIGATOR SEA CABIN, CHART HOUSE, COMMS. STORE, SIGNAL DECK, K, J, A, B, C, E, D, I, C, F, G, W.C., H, H, N, **Starboard**

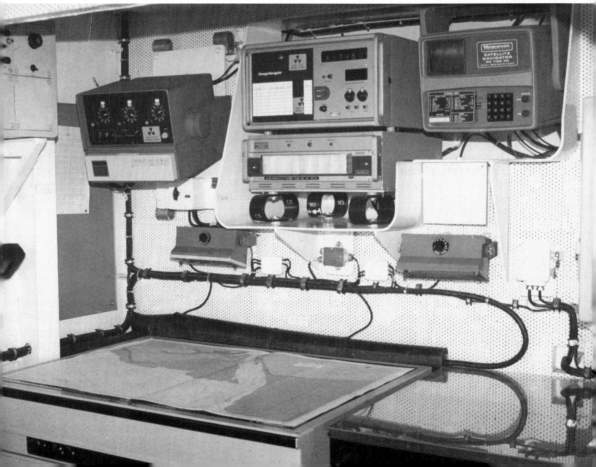

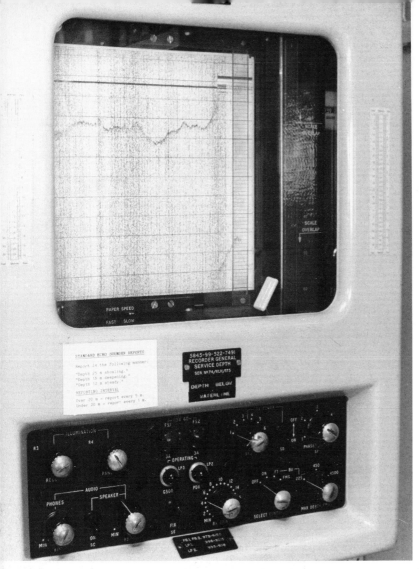

Left:
The chart recorder for the Type 778 Depth Finder.

very low frequencies (VLF). It comes into its own on longer passages and in parts of the world where Decca coverage is limited or non-existent. In contrast to Decca, the ship's position is shown as a latitude and longitude on a LED readout incorporated into the control panel, and this can then be manually plotted on the chart.

For satellite navigation the ship is fitted with a standard Magnavox MX1102RN which has been in service with the RN for many years and utilises the US Navy's TRANSIT satellite navigation system. This consists of a number of satellites circling the earth in polar orbits, each orbit taking 107min. At worst, every point of the earth will be covered at least once every 24hr enabling an accurate position fix to be obtained. However, in practice most areas will have considerably better coverage and a fix can be obtained around every 15min in many parts of the North Atlantic.

In operation, the satellite transmits a burst of information every 2min on two frequencies (150MHz and 400MHz) allowing the shipboard equipment to detect errors due to ionospheric refraction by means of Doppler shift. Using information from three successive transmissions, the equipment can give position with accuracy measured in only tens of metres.

The Type 778 Depth Finder is old but reliable equipment and a continuous moving chart displays depth under the keel to a high degree of accuracy. Housed in a cabinet to the right of the chart table, it also drives the depth indicator on the OOW's panel at the front of the Bridge.

One of the most important of the navigation systems is not immediately apparent. This is SINS – or Ship's Inertial Navigation System – which utilises a gyro-based inertial platform similar in principle to systems commonly used in aircraft navigation. The master controls for this are situated in the chart house abaft the Bridge, but information from the system can be accessed at the chart table by means of SNAPS – Ship's Navigation and Processing System. Using this a display of the ship's position, as calculated by SINS, is shown by a moving reticule projected from below on to the glass surface of the chart table. Once the ship's position has been accurately determined by other means, such as Decca or a visual fix, SINS will then cause the reticule to move beneath the chart to correspond to the movement of the ship. Illumination of the reticule can be adjusted so that it clearly shows through the chart.

In order to cope with this type of input, the chart table is more than just a surface on which to rest charts and carry out conventional navigational plotting with pencil, rulers and dividers. It is in fact only part of the SNAPS which comprises four separate units: a computer, a data logger, a combined keyboard and display unit, and the chart table itself. Although mechanical plotting tables are nothing new (the first were installed well before World War 1) their use has required careful setting up and monitoring, particularly when changing to a new chart which will almost certainly be of a different scale. With SNAPS, as a new chart is used, it is only necessary to move the reticule to any three points on the chart and enter the latitude and longitude of each position into the system by means of the handheld keyboard/display unit. SNAPS then automatically calculates the scale,

projection and orientation of the chart. With an initial fix entered, the system will then automatically track the ship's position using inputs from Omega, Decca, SINS or the SatNav. In addition it can be updated by entering a visually-derived position by means of the keyboard. As successive position fixes are entered into SNAPS the accuracy of the system increases. Conversely, if regular updates are not fed in then the computer-derived position will gradually lose accuracy. For naval purposes it is essential that an accurate position is maintained at all times and consequently no single method is relied upon exclusively but, instead, a continuous process of cross-checking is employed using two or more of the methods available. In this context it is worth noting that many of the sophisticated aids such as Decca or satellites may not be available through jamming or enemy action in time of hostilities, so that the value of maintaining proficiency in more traditional methods of navigation will be apparent. Thus an Officer Under Training will still be seen taking the traditional noon sighting with a sextant.

The array of navigation equipment is rounded off by a second Type 1006 radar display standing on its own just to the left of the chart table.

Below:
The handheld SNAPS keyboard allows the OOW to access and display information from the Ship's Inertial Navigation System (SINS).

However, there is one further radar console on the Bridge and this is situated, facing aft, on the port side immediately abaft the Captain's chair. Again, this is a piece of equipment which shows that this is a warship's Bridge. The picture on the screen is not intended for navigational purposes but instead shows information on all targets detected by the ship's sensors, including aircraft and submarines, as well as other ships. Compilation of the picture and labelling of targets is done in the Operations Room below decks using inputs to the ADAWS computer. In a threat environment the Captain will normally move to the Operations Room where he has full facilities to observe the situation and carry out his Command function. However, there may be occasions when he will wish to do this from the Bridge and the picture provided on the ADAWS display enables him to achieve this. Even if the Captain is below, the provision of a tactical display on the Bridge allows the OOW to keep a check on the current situation so that he can

anticipate future developments as they affect the handling of the ship.

Although the foregoing paragraphs will have given a comprehensive view of the Bridge – or Compass Platform – and its equipment, it does not give a complete picture of the organisation necessary for the direction of the ship. At 04 Deck Level where the Bridge is situated are a number of other compartments which are directly related to the Conduct of the ship and her aircraft.

As the prime purpose of an aircraft carrier is to carry and operate its aircraft, it is obvious that the conduct of flying operations cannot be divorced from the operation of the ship. The actual utilisation of the flightdeck and control of aircraft taking off and landing is run from the Flying Control (Flyco) cabin formed by an aft extension of the port wing of the Bridge. Here, facing aft with an excellent view over the flightdeck, sits the Lieutenant Commander (Flying) otherwise known as Little 'F' who is responsible for running the flying operations on the deck. Behind him is normally the ship's Commander (Air) who in turn is responsible to the Captain for all aspects of the air activity aboard the ship. A third member of the Flyco team is the Logger, a communications rating who mans a

Below:
Aft of the Bridge, on the port side, is the Flyco cabin from where flying operations are conducted. This view of Flyco is looking aft from the Bridge.

console arranged along the port side. A more detailed description of Flyco and its method of working is given in a following chapter.

Access to the Bridge deck is by means of a staircase which leads up to a lobby on the starboard side. From here a hatchway opens directly on to the starboard wing of the Bridge, while a cross-passage runs behind the Bridge to lead into the Flyco cabin. On the after side of this passage are the Navigating Officer's Sea Cabin and the Chart House. The ship's Navigating Officer, variously known as the Navigator or Pilot, is directly responsible to the Captain for all matters concerning the safe navigation and handling of the ship. Apart from ensuring that the ship's watchkeeping officers and OUTs are maintaining a satisfactory standard, he must also ensure that all charts are kept up to date and is also responsible for forward and long term planning of the ship's movements. In order to be constantly on hand to assist and support the watchkeepers while the ship is at sea, he has his own sea cabin situated immediately adjacent to

the Bridge. Facilities are very basic and comprise a desk and locker with a bunk mounted on top plus a chair. Although he has a larger cabin more appropriate to his rank (Lt-Cdr) situated aft, he rarely sees it while at sea.

The chart house is the Navigator's working office where the ship's library of charts and navigational documents is stored, as only those charts actually relevant to the ship's current area of operations are kept on the Bridge by the chart table. Thus, while the ship is currently steaming in the Irish Sea, the Navigator is working on a chart showing the approaches to Vigo in northern Spain for a visit planned two months ahead. After that he will look to the charts for a major deployment to the Western Atlantic at the end of the year. Above his head a panel contains a telephone keyboard and repeaters of the log and compass so that he can keep an eye on the current situation. In addition, and more significantly, he has access to a keypad and VDU for operating the ship's SINS.

Alongside the lobby at the top of the staircase is a toilet, a vital installation given the number of men normally on the Bridge for long periods. Aft of the lobby a watertight door leads out on to the open Flag Signal Deck where a locker contains the

Below:
The Navigating Officer at work in the Chart House. Above his head is the keyboard panel to access SINS.

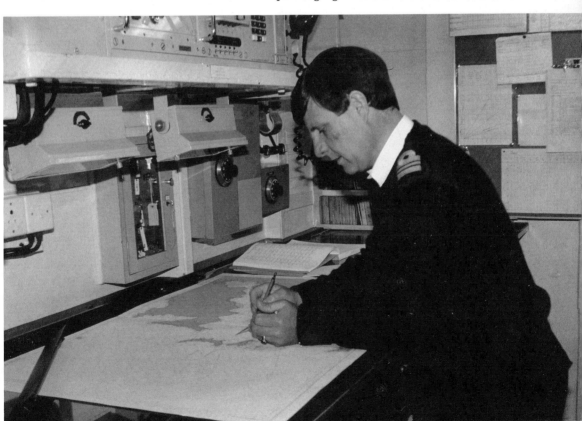

Above:
Situated immediately below the Bridge is the Captain's sea cabin where he can work in private, but where he is instantly available should his presence be required. He can communicate with the Bridge by means of a two-way intercom.

various flags and hoists, and the halyards running up to the cross-tree on the foremast can be reached. An external ladder leads up to the Signal Bridge on the roof of the Compass Platform.

On the deck below the Main Bridge, 3 Deck, is the Captain's sea cabin where he is available on call at all times when not actually on the Bridge or in the Operations Room (which is reached by a small lift) during the periods when the ship is at sea. Also on this deck level is a cabin for the Commander (Air) and moving down one further level is a small mess used by him and the Navigating Officer for meals. A small galley and a toilet are situated at the after end of this flat. The galley serves the small mess and is also used by the Captain's steward to prepare his meals. At the fore end is an enclosed gallery which externally appears to be a smaller version of the Main Bridge above. However, this platform has little in the way of instrumentation and only basic communications facilities. It is intended for use

by an Admiral and his staff when they are embarked and provides a facility for them to watch operations without interfering with the routine running of the ship. With no Admiral aboard at present, the Captain is able to use it as a meeting area for his daily Command briefings held with the ship's heads of department.

From the foregoing description it will be realised that the Bridge, and the officers and cabins surrounding it, are a self-contained world remote from the rest of the ship. While the ship is at sea, only those members of the crew whose duties are concerned with the running of the Bridge will actually climb the several staircases leading up from 2 Deck, and some officers will go nowhere else. It is as well at this point to look at the responsibilities of those concerned with the running of the ship. The Captain, of course, has complete responsibility for all matters concerning the ship and is termed to have 'Command'. As such he is deemed to be responsible for all that happens aboard and, therefore, he requires that the OOW should keep him informed at all times of proposed actions so that he can consider, amend if necessary, and approve these.

To assist him in the discharge of his duties, the Captain is supported by his team of officers — particularly the heads of the various departments who accept responsibility for their part of the ship's organisation. The day-to-day administration of the ship and the maintenance of good order and discipline is carried out by the ship's Executive Officer or Commander, Cdr Peter Booth. He, along with the Commander (Air) and Navigating Officer, is one of three officers to whom the Captain can delegate 'Conduct' of the ship. This means that they, through their experience and qualifications, can be responsible for the way in which the ship carries out her assigned tasks, being totally responsible for the navigation of the ship and the operation of her aircraft, weapons and equipment without direct reference to the Captain, although they remain responsible to him for their actions.

It is essential that the officer having Conduct of the ship should be in the immediate vicinity of the Bridge or the operations room at all times and this is why the Navigator and Commander (Air) have sea cabins in the Bridge superstructure along with the Captain. The exception to this is the Commander who retains his suite of cabins aft, even while at sea, enabling him to carry out his executive functions and maintain the disciplined routine of the ship.

The officer having Conduct of the ship will delegate still further to the Officer of the Watch who is said to have 'Charge'. During his period of Watch the OOW will be responsible (among other things) for: the passage of the ship; ensuring its safe navigation and keeping the chart plot up to date; taking such action as is necessary to maintain the safety of the ship including altering course and speed as necessary to avoid collision with other vessels; keeping the ship in the correct station relative to other ships sailing in company, and manoeuvring to allow the operation of weapons and aircraft as directed by the Captain or one of the officers having Conduct. The OOW is normally a lieutenant or senior sub-lieutenant and is assisted by a Second Officer of the Watch known, logically enough, as the 'Second'. The latter is normally a sub-lieutenant or a midshipman and is often an OUT who is working towards his watchkeeping certificate.

Despite having 'Charge' of the ship, the OOW will normally only deal with the most routine affairs without consultation. For anything in the least out of the ordinary he will report the situation to the Captain (or the officer having Conduct) together with his appreciation and proposed course of action. Only after this has been approved will he carry on. Of course, there are times when circumstances will demand that he acts first and reports afterwards. This could include a man-overboard situation or the detection of an incoming torpedo where any delay could cause the loss of lives or the ship. An example of this occurred in the Falklands where the OOW aboard the 'County' class destroyer HMS *Glamorgan* almost certainly saved the ship and reduced the casualties on board when he made a prompt alteration of course to bring the ship stern-on to an approaching Exocet missile fired from a shore launcher. Fortunately, such action is rarely required in peacetime.

Under normal circumstances (Cruising Stations) the Bridge team comprises the OOW and his Second, a quartermaster, a senior communications rating with a radio operator assisting, and the Bosun's Mate. At night this is increased by two ratings to act as lookouts. The officer having Conduct will be readily available and the Captain may well be present. To ensure that all concerned are fresh and alert, the Watches are regularly changed in a pattern of working which has stood the test of time in the Royal Navy. With slight variation, the day is split into four-hour periods known as Watches. From midnight to 0400 is the Middle, followed by the Morning from 0400-0800. Aboard *Invincible* the Forenoon Watch is extended by half-an-hour so that it runs from 0800-1230 and the subsequent Afternoon Watch consequently runs from 1230-1600. This variation is deemed more convenient for messing arrangements at lunch. The four-hour period from 1600-2000 is actually split into two short two-hour Watches known as the first and last Dog Watches and the four hours to midnight constitute the First Watch.

The Dog Watches were introduced into the system in order to give an odd number of Watches in the day so that crew working the standard one-on-and-two-off system did not work the same periods on successive days. With the number of officers including OUTs available in *Invincible*, most Bridge watchkeepers work one-in-four or even one-in-five.

This basic routine will be overridden on various occasions. The procedure for leaving harbour has already been described and similar arrangements apply for entering a harbour and berthing alongside. Flying operations involve the manning of Flyco while various exercises and evolutions will bring additional specialists, lookouts, and signallers to the Bridge. At Action Stations the air of drama is heightened as anti-flash gear — consisting of white cotton hoods, facemasks and gloves — is donned.

However, at Cruising Stations the atmosphere is one of relaxed competence. There is time to chat and, on warm pleasant days, reflect that you are actually being paid for the pleasure of conning one of Britain's most powerful warships across a placid sea. Unfortunately, the Royal Navy has centuries of experience in ensuring that such peaceful moments do not last and every day brings another range of exercises and serials.

FLYING OPERATIONS

Thursday Afternoon

After clearing Portsmouth and the Solent, *Invincible* arrives at the RV point for the embarkation of her Air Group consisting of Sea Harrier jet fighters and Sea King helicopters. By 1230, as the first four Sea Harriers (referred to aboard ship as SHARs) of 800 NAS roar overhead in a neat echelon formation, the flightdeck has been cleared and the ship is at Flying Stations. Under instructions from Little 'F', sitting high up overlooking the deck from his cabin abaft the Bridge, the four aircraft turn in to approach over the port side of the ship for vertical landings on the designated deck spots at 30sec intervals. As soon as all four are down, the flightdeck directors in their yellow jackets wave directions to the pilots indicating their parking spots. Two of the

SHARs are taxied forward and secured in the deck park forward of the Bridge while the rear two, amazingly, taxy backwards to their spots on the stern.

A few minutes of hectic activity leave the landing spots clear again as the next wave of four SHARs flash overhead and turn downwind to position for landing on. All four were soon on deck with only 90sec separating the first and last touchdown. This time two aircraft are moved to the after deck park while the forward pair are quickly towed to the fore and aft lifts where they are struck down to the hangar below.

The last SHAR lands at 1240 and 2min later the Sea Kings are approaching the ship from the northwest in a formation of seven aircraft made up of six Sea King HAS5s from 814 NAS and a lone Sea King AEW2 of 849 NAS. As with the Sea Harriers, the Sea Kings are designated in

Left:
The Air Group embarks – Sea Harriers of 800 NAS come to the hover over *Invincible's* flightdeck.

Above:
With the Sea Harriers safely secured on the stern deck park, two Sea Kings of 814 NAS approach the ship's port side for landing.

abbreviated form where SKJ refers to the ASW versions and SKW — or Whiskey — to the AEW variant with its bulky side-mounted radome. The first four SKJs commence landing on at 1248 and by 1252 all are on deck with their engines shut down and rotors spinning to a stop. Before moving the helicopters it is necessary to fold and secure the rotors, a procedure which takes about 5min so that it is 1258 before the first SKJ is being towed to a parking position close up against the port side of the island superstructure.

As the deck is cleared, the last two SKJs land on, followed a few minutes later by the SKW. All three are then secured on deck, but initially left parked on their landing spots. The ship remains at flying stations until 1328 when all 15 aircraft (8 SHAR, 6 SKJ, 1 SKW) have been embarked and secured. Although the ship's normal complement is 20, the shortfall has been caused by the fact that three of the 814 SKJs and two of 849's SKWs were undergoing maintenance checks at the time of embarkation and are therefore scheduled to join the ship at a later date in time for operational deployments.

With her air group safely aboard, *Invincible* sails towards her exercise areas off Portland to carry out a series of tests and trials before continuing on her scheduled training voyage around the UK. Already, as soon as the ship is secured from flying stations, the Operations Room team commence a series of firing drills for the GWS30 Sea Dart surface-to-air missile system. Although the whole operation is conducted from below decks, the OOW is involved as he is able to confirm to the firing team that the deck around the launcher is clear for firing, and visually check that the launcher has loaded, trained and elevated correctly.

At 1420 the ship again goes briefly to Flying Stations to allow a shore-based Sea King HC4 to land aboard, bringing the last of the squadron personnel and their baggage. Unloading is carried out with rotors running and the green-painted Sea King lifts off again at 1440, turning left to pass behind the ship before setting course for RNAS Yeovilton, from where the embarking squadrons have departed.

Aboard *Invincible*, the routine of checks and trials continue with a test of the underwater telephone system carried out in conjunction with the Type 22 frigate HMS *London* several miles away. Later in the afternoon the two ships close to carry out an intelligence-gathering exercise. In this scenario each ship assumes that the other is a Soviet ship and attempts to glean as much information as possible by visual observation and electronic monitoring while at the same time attempting to hide or disguise its own equipment and methods of operation.

This evolution gives a lot of scope for imagination and initiative, some serious and some lighthearted. Aboard *Invincible* the ship's intelligence officer (SHINTO) briefs his team on what to look for and advises the Captain on what steps should be taken to avoid giving away too much to the other ship. *London* has launched a Lynx helicopter. Aboard *Invincible*, video came-ras are trained on *London* and the Lynx while the Bridge team attempt to identify what appears to be a clutch of new aerials above the frigate's Bridge. After a while it becomes apparent that *London* is attempting to hide her port side from observation and so the two ships twist and turn as *Invincible* attempts to circle round and find out what the other ship is trying to hide — a difficult situation as the frigate is obviously more manoeuvrable. Eventually an unexpected turn reveals that *London* has succeeded in launching and recovering a boat for some unknown purpose.

Meanwhile, the crew of *London's* Lynx are attracted by a civilian operating what appears to be some sophisticated equipment on *Invincible's* Flag Bridge. The civilian is taking obvious pains to try and avoid observation and causes the helicopter crew some difficulty as they fly very close. In fact the 'civilian' is one of *Invincible's* crew and his equipment is no more than a wooden box fitted with a stick surmounted by a hair curler and with a pair of 'Walkman' headphones 'plugged in'! No doubt *London's* aerials are a similar ruse but such tricks provide excellent training in observation techniques.

Below:
A shore-based Sea King HC4 lifts off from the crowded flightdeck after delivering last-minute supplies and personnel.

As a final spoof, both ships are flying incongruous flag signals. *London* has two large yellow flags prominently hoisted — the international quarantine flags indicating a serious infectious illness on board — while *Invincible* has included her Pusser's Rum pennant among a colourful display of bunting.

The exercise ends at 1700 and the ships part company with *Invincible's* Marine Engineering department taking advantage of a quiet period to carry out machinery drills below. By 1900 these are complete as the ship RVs with the RFA *Gold Rover* for a RAS serial. RAS, or Replenishment at Sea, is the means by which a warship can take on stores, fuel and ammunition from a supply ship or tanker whilst underway at sea and is a vital and indispensable part of modern naval operations.

On this occasion *Invincible* has only just left Portsmouth and is fully stored (except for ammunition supplies which will be taken on in a few days time), but the exercises have been planned to allow the ship to test her RAS gear before proceeding away from the area, and to give the Bridge team some useful practice. Over the next 3hr the two ships carry out a number of RAS procedures although the first is abandoned due to a fault on one of *Invincible's* hoists. The ships

Above:
HMS *London*, a Batch 2 Type 22 frigate, comes alongside *Invincible* during an intelligence-gathering exercise. The frigate carries an interesting array of aerials atop the deckhouse abaft the Bridge and is flying the yellow quarantine flag on the foremast yardarms.

Below:
To provide a talking point for observers on the frigate, *Invincible* hoists a Russian naval ensign together with the Pusser's Rum pennant.

disengage while this is fixed and then the lines are passed again. This time everything works perfectly and a number of test loads are passed back and forth using both the fore and aft jackstays. Finally *Invincible* closes up for a final exercise and a fuel line is passed from the RFA allowing the carrier to top up her fuel bunkers before breaking off and setting course to the west at 2220.

The day's exercises — having been almost continuous — are now complete, and *Invincible* heads down channel to pass around the south-west tip of Cornwall before heading north into the Irish Sea where she is due to carry out flying exercises off the Welsh coast the following morning. To reach her allotted area, she must make a fast passage and speed is increased to 22kt as the crew fall out to Cruising Stations and those not on Watch settle down to snatch a few hours sleep.

Friday

Dawn on Friday finds the ship on a course of 005° having passed into the Irish Sea during the night and now heading for her new exercise area approximately 50 miles southwest of St Ann's Head on the Pembrokeshire coast. The weather conditions are excellent for the day's flying programme — a fresh northeasterly breeze is forecast to moderate and back to northwesterly while the broken cloud layer is expected to disperse later in the day. The sea is calm and visibility is good.

On the Bridge there is a bustle of activity as the Watch changes and the Flyco team close up. The Captain is also present, seated on the port side as the OOW instructs the Bosun's Mate to pipe Flying Stations. The routine call echoes over the ship's broadcast system:

'Hands to Flying Stations, Hands to Flying Stations. No gash to be ditched. Access to flightdeck is to via one Lima ACR only.'

It is important that only authorised crew members are on the flightdeck during flying operations so that all access to it is closed off except for the lobby at 1 Lima which leads out from the centre of the island superstructure. Alongside this lobby is the Aircraft Control Room (ACR) where the duty PO controls access to the deck. The ACR is also responsible for keeping track of where all the ship's aircraft are parked or hangared and, working in conjunction with Flyco and the Flight Deck Director, are responsible for determining the movement of aircraft around the ship so that they are correctly situated for their part in the flying programme. With up to 20 aircraft aboard and only limited hangar and parking space, this can be a complex task. In general terms the hangar is reserved for aircraft undergoing major maintenance or repair, or for parking aircraft not likely to be involved in the day's flying programme.

On deck the SHARs are normally ranged aft as they require a certain amount of forward run for take-off, while the helicopters — which always take-off vertically — are usually parked forward or alongside the island from where they can use the forward section of the flightdeck. To assist the positioning of aircraft, the deck has various markings painted on including a broad black

Left:
A view of *Gold Rover* from *Invincible's* Bridge as the two ships close for a RAS serial.

Above:
**A view from the bows as *Invincible* steams at Flying
Stations in the Irish Sea. A Sea King HAS5 is landing on
amidships and the upward curve of the ski-jump ramp
is visible on the right.**

Left:
**Flying operations are co-ordinated from the Flying
Control cabin (Flyco) immediately abaft the Bridge. The
officer in charge, known as Little 'F', has direct
communications with the pilots, flightdeck parties, the
aircraft control room and the Bridge.**

stripe running the whole length and leading up to
the ski-jump ramp forward. This shows the
centreline of the SHAR's take-off run and is also
used by the helicopters to align themselves fore
and aft for landings and take-offs. At approximately 100ft intervals along this line are the
figures 1, 2, 3 and 4 which indicate the landing
spots normally used by all aircraft for vertical
landings, while right aft on the port side are
spots 6 and 8 with spots 5, 7 and 9 marked out on

the starboard side aft. These latter points are very closely spaced and are normally used for parking only.

Overall control of aircraft movements on the flightdeck is vested in the Flyco officer (Little 'F'), but he must work closely with the ACR and, more importantly, the Flightdeck Officer (FDO) who is actually on the deck and controls his team of directors who marshall and direct the aircraft by hand signals. Communication between Flyco and the FDO is by means of an open circuit induction loop system. The loop runs around the edge of the flightdeck and transmissions from Flyco are fed to the loop and picked up by a receiver in the FDO's helmet. He, in turn, speaks to Flyco through a low-powered transmitter attached to his boom microphone, the signals from which are picked up by the loop. The FDO is an extremely important member of the team and his word is law on the flightdeck. He will advise Flyco when aircraft are ready to be moved and will also report when landing spots have been cleared and are ready to receive aircraft. In addition, no personnel will be allowed on the deck without his permission and are subject to his orders at all times.

During Flying Stations there are several categories of crew working on the deck — each visibly distinguished by different coloured tabards. The FDO and his directors — who are responsible for marshalling and directing air-craft on deck — wear yellow, while the naval airmen who drive the tractors, refuel and secure the aircraft to the deck are distinguished by the colour blue. The variety of specialists who maintain the aircraft are distinguished by red for armourers, brown for mechanical maintainers (eg engine fitters), green for electrical trades and checked green and blue for radio mechanics. White with a black stripe indicates the flightdeck engineers who are universally known as 'Badgers', while the medical team wear the traditional red cross. Almost everybody wears blue overalls, although officers are distinguished by white overalls. Ear defenders are worn by all personnel and sleeves must be rolled down to cover arms at all times.

The flightdeck is an extremely dangerous place and tight control coupled with a high standard of training and discipline is essential to its safe operation. Anybody who has ever seen and heard a Sea Harrier hovering perhaps 100yd away at an airshow will be able to imagine the incredible noise generated by three or four SHARs hovering only a few feet away as they come into land, blasting the flightdeck with eddying gusts of hot

Left:
To assist the functioning of Flyco, a communications rating – the Logger – looks after routine telephone calls and records all flightdeck take-offs and landings.

Below:
A Sea Harrier lands on, watched by a flightdeck director and aircraft handlers. Note the firefighter in the foreground.
HMS Illustrious *Photographic Section*

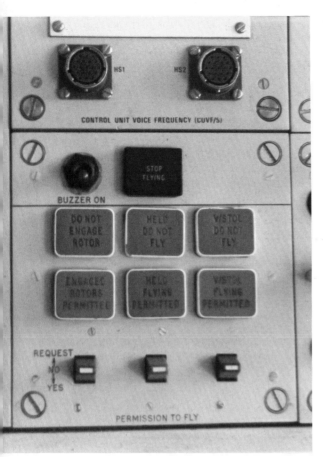

Above:

The panel on the Flyco console used to co-ordinate flying operations with the Bridge. The top row of three square lights are red while the lower row are green. These will be selected and illuminated from the Captain's console on the Bridge, depending on the status of flying operations permitted.

air from the roaring Pegasus engines. Helicopter rotor blades skim round only feet from the superstructure, just above head level. In bad weather the ship will be pitching and rolling and rain, spray and even ice can make the deck surface slippery and treacherous. To a casual observer it is a miracle that order can be brought to this apparent chaos. Although helicopters and STOVL have made the actual take-off and landings less risky than was the case with conventional aircraft, it should be borne in mind that HMS *Invincible* is considerably smaller than earlier aircraft carriers such as the previous *Ark Royal* and deck space is at a premium.

On this sunny Friday the weather conditions are favourable for a busy morning's FLYEX (Flying Exercise). Already, before the ship was

called to Flying Stations, the first waves of aircraft have been ranged on deck with three SKJs occupying spots 1, 2 and 3 while the sole SKW and five SHARs are clustered right aft. In Flyco, Lt-Cdr Alan Smith looks down and checks that everything is ready to commence flying operations while at the same time the FDO calls to report that the SKJs are ready to start engines, their rotors having already been unfolded and spread.

In the period leading up to the start of flying operations, Little 'F' will have checked the wind over the deck (WOD) parameters required for the operation of the various aircraft types to be flown. On the starboard bulkhead of the Flyco cabin are pasted charts showing the maximum acceptable WOD from all directions, relative to the flight deck axis, and these will be variable depending on the actual weight of the aircraft. For example the SHARs can normally accept a light wind up to 40° off the bow, but at heavy all-up weights this is reduced to only 15°, restricting the ship's freedom to manoeuvre. This is important as, especially when operating as part of a task force, tactical considerations may require the ship to head in one direction but achieving a suitable WOD will require a major change of course. Thus the ship's Commander (Air), Little 'F' and the OOW will negotiate and decide on the most suitable course to be steered during flying operations and this is known as the Designated Flying Course (DFC). Given a specified WOD, the OOW uses a calculator — made up of a clear perspex compass rose mounted so that it can be rotated and slid over a calibrated angular scale engraved on a second piece of perspex — to work out suitable combinations of courses and speeds for the ship. Subsequently he will ensure that the ship comes on to the DFC and speed is adjusted for the requisite WOD at the time specified for the commencement of flying operations. In today's conditions the ship is able to maintain her northerly course, and a steady 8kt gives 20kt wind straight down the deck. Flyco can monitor the relative wind speed and direction from instruments on the panel in front of him, while ship's course and speed are repeated on the deckhead panels above him.

With everything ready to go he reaches forward and presses one of three switches situated at the lower left-hand corner of his console. These switches are immediately below two rows of three backlit indicators, the top row red and all illuminated at present, and the lower row green. Depressing the left-hand switch illuminates a warning light on the Captain's console alongside a similar array of indicators, as well as sounding a buzzer. The Captain or the OOW replies by switching the left-hand indicator from red to

The Flyco Team

The Flyco Team

COMMANDER (AIR) A ship's officer, otherwise known as 'Wings', responsible to the Captain for all aspects of air operations and is normally on the Bridge while the ship is at Flying Stations. Authorised to have Conduct of the ship.

LITTLE 'F' The traditional name for the Flying Control Officer who is normally a Lt-Cdr by rank. He is responsible to the Commander (Air) for the safe conduct of aircraft operations aboard ship while the ship is at Flying Stations. His duties involve close co-ordination with the Captain and OOW.

LOGGER A rating who runs the Flyco telephone switchboard and maintains a record of events including a log of aircraft arrivals and departures.

the flightdeck who, by means of hand signals, indicate that it is safe to do so.

Very quickly the Sea Kings spool up their twin turboshaft engines. The pilots can talk directly to Flyco through telebrief telephone lines, still connected to the aircraft at this point, and report engines running, ready to engage rotors. This requires a quick check that the WOD is within limits to avoid the initially slow moving blades waving about and striking the aircraft's tail-boom. With this done an amber traffic light is selected — indicating to the crews on the flightdeck that it is safe to spread or engage rotors. Slowly at first, but quickly accelerating, the five-bladed rotors begin to turn and are soon just a circular blur. A few minutes pass while pilots complete their cockpit checks and then signal to the directors that they are ready. Up to this point each helicopter is firmly lashed to the deck by four webbing straps.

With the rotors running, Flyco will have pressed a second switch and received back a green to indicate Captain's approval for helicopter flying to commence. The traffic lights turn to green and the pilots have a 'Green Deck'. With three SKJs ranged on the 1, 2 and 3 spots, take-off is in reverse order with the Sea King on 3 spot

green, and this repeated on Little 'F's' panel signifies that aircraft on deck are cleared to start engines and engage rotors. This in turn is relayed to the deck by means of 'traffic lights' located on the superstructure below the Flyco cabin. On getting the green from the Bridge, Flyco selects a red traffic light which signifies to the pilots in their cockpits that they are cleared to start engines and this confirmed by the directors on

Below:
A Sea King prepares for take-off. The naval airman standing by the aircraft's side is awaiting a signal from the flightdeck director in the foreground to release the webbing lashing which still secures the helicopter to the deck.

Above:
Take-off. A Sea King lifts off and pulls away to port to clear the deck.

going first. As soon as the pilot signals that he is ready to go, the flightdeck director in turn moves his hands in a rotary wrapping motion to indicate to the airman standing by the lashings to disconnect them. As this is done they coil the webbing straps up and stand in a row beside the yellow-jacketed director, holding the lashings out so that the pilot can visually confirm that they have all been released and accounted for. One of the airmen will also have unplugged the telebrief lead. A nod from the pilot acknowledges all this and the airmen move clear while he calls Flyco on the prebriefed UHF radio channel.

Flyco 'Victor Five Sierra, cleared to lift.'

The pilot gives a thumbs up to the flightdeck director who lifts his arms in confirmation that it is safe to lift off; as soon as the heavy Sea King's wheels leave the deck he points out to port with both arms. The pilot then edges the helicopter sideways until clear of the ship, turns about 15° to the left and transitions forward to climb away from the ship. It is all over in a few seconds and the second and third SKJs quickly follow from 2 and 1 spots respectively, all three airborne by 0812.

Once the three helicopters are safely airborne the traffic lights are extinguished and the Captain cancels the Permission to Fly light. However, this still leaves Little 'F' free to move aircraft on the deck, start engines and engage rotors as required. In the meantime the three helicopters have left Flyco's radio frequency and are now in contact

with the ship's air traffic controllers, known as Homer, working in the Operations Room below. Their radio calls can, if required, be monitored from Flyco by selecting one of 16 buttons corresponding to the preselected radio frequency.

After the three Sea Kings are all airborne, the next to take-off will be the AEW Sea King. As soon as the deck is clear, the 'Whiskey' is released from its securing chains and towed by a small tractor down the deck to spot 2 where it is secured again by webbing straps. The rotors are spread and the crew carry our their pre-flight checks. Once ready, engines are started and the rotor engaged under the watchful eye of a flightdeck director. Flyco requests permission to commence flying again and receives the appropriate green light on his panel from the Captain. Changing the 'traffic light' to green, he gives take-off permission over the radio and the SKW with its bulky radar installation is waved off the deck by the director at precisely 0830.

The next range of aircraft will be four SHARs due off at 0910. With a lull in proceedings all lights are extinguished and, if required, the OOW would now be free to turn the ship off the flying course and alter speed. Today however, *Invincible* maintains her northerly course, creeping along at a steady 8kt. After completing an external check of the aircraft, the SHAR pilots climb into their cockpits and run through the

Above:
A Sea Harrier leaps into the air from the ski-jump ramp on the ship's bows. Use of a short take-off run and the ramp allows the aircraft to operate at considerably heavier weights than would be the case with a normal or vertical take-off.

pre-flight drills, calling to Flyco on the telebrief when ready to start engines. Here a similar procedure to that adopted for the helicopter departures is carried out, but this time the traffic light signals to the deck have a slightly different meaning. Red indicates that engines can be started and run, amber gives permission to taxi, and green is take-off clearance. The amber light is also used during recoveries to indicate that the deck is cleared for the SHARs to land on.

With engines running the lead pilot, callsign 'Red Leader', checks in on the radio and advises Flyco that the formation is ready to go. An amber light shines down and the aircraft handlers release the chain lashings on the first aircraft. It is led forward by signals from one of the flightdeck directors to a spot on the black runway centreline, just forward of the after lift. A green light from Flyco, the director steps clear and waves the aircraft away, the pilot spools up the powerful Pegasus engine and the SHAR accelerates away down the deck and up over the ski-jump at the bows. For a moment the aircraft appears to hang in the air as the upward momentum imparted by the ramp fades away and is replaced by aerodynamic lift and engine thrust as speed increases.

Already the second aircraft, Red 2, has moved forward and is waved away, closely followed by the last pair. In just over a minute all four aircraft are airborne, climbing away to the northwest and changing frequency to call Homer. It is now 0912 and *Invincible* has eight of her aircraft airborne, but there is no respite for the busy flightdeck

parties: already the three SKJs launched an hour ago are returning.

Their return has already been heralded to Flyco by a call on the open intercom line from the air traffic controller in the Operations Room. In bad weather the controller can bring the aircraft into visual contact with the ship by using information derived from his radar screen. If necessary, he can even give them a talkdown to put the aircraft or helicopter close alongside the ship for a landing in poor visibility. In today's clear weather such procedures are not required and the helicopters are in visual contact from many miles out. As the last of the SHARs is airborne, the three helicopters are approaching the ship's port quarter in a strung-out line. Flyco has already advised the FDO of the inbound SKJs and, in return, has been told that they are to land on spots 2, 3 and 4.

At each spot stands a yellow-jacketed director ready to guide the helicopter as it lands. They look up towards Flyco and check that the deck is still 'green' as the first of the arrivals comes into the hover off the ship's port beam. The director on 2 spot waves his Sea King in over the deck and gives the land signal — arms outstretched and palms pushed down — as the helicopter inches

***Invincible* normally operates three Sea King AEW2 helicopters of 849 NAS and one of these is shown landing on 4 Spot by the after hangar lift.**

into the correct position. As soon as the wheels are firmly on the deck, the aircraft handlers move in and secure their lashings while the rotor is still running. The other two Sea Kings follow quickly in turn and the flightdeck is a hive of activity as the rear pair are refuelled and taken over by new crews for a further sortie — all done with engines and rotors running. In 10min the work is done and the two grey-painted SKJs lift off to port and move away from 'Mother' (as the ship is invariably referred to among the aircrew). The third SKJ has developed a technical fault and while the others are being turned round its engines have been shut down and rotors folded. Once the deck is free it is towed clear and parked alongside the island.

It is now 0945 and there is a short lull in flightdeck operations as four RAF Hawk aircraft, operating from Brawdy in southwest Wales, carry out mock attacks on the ship to exercise the Operations Room team. On the Bridge the OOW keeps a sharp eye out for other vessels as the ship carries out several sharp changes of course under

the directions of the PWO to evade attack, and to give the onboard weapon systems clear arcs of fire. As the Hawks bore in at low level on the starboard side, the ship's Goalkeeper CIWS mountings can be observed relentlessly tracking the fast-moving targets.

After two mock attacks, the Hawks reform and circle the ship before diving across the stern to carry out live firing runs at a splash target towed two cables astern. Each run consists of a shallow dive and a short burst, less than half a second, from their underslung 30mm gun pods. Each time, the sea around the target boils under the lash of hundreds of cannon shells. After three or four runs, each aircraft has exhausted its ammunition and the four aircraft reform again before making a spectacular low level pass up the port side of the ship and then pulling up and breaking right to set course back to Brawdy.

Once the Hawks have gone, preparations are made to recover the four SHARs of Red Section which have now been airborne for over an hour. Under direction from Homer, the aircraft are running in fast from the southwest and Flyco's speaker crackles into life as they check in.

Flyco 'Mother, Red Section slotting in two minutes.'

superstructure, abaft the Bridge and Flyco, is mounted a landing sight which indicates to the pilot the correct approach path to the ship. Each aircraft follows a similar procedure to the helicopters, coming to the hover off the port side of the ship and edging in some 20ft above the deck. On a signal from one of the directors, the pilot reduces power and allows the aircraft to sink quickly and very firmly on to the deck, avoiding problems caused by hovering low down in the recirculating hot exhaust gases.

The first SHAR touches down on spot 2 and is immediately waved forward by the director to make room for the second aircraft which also uses spot 2. The last two are waved on to spots 3 and 4. With all four down, the front aircraft is waved forward into the deck park immediately

Slotting refers to the procedure where aircraft join the ship for landing approach in formation from astern, fly up the starboard side of the ship before breaking off individually to port, across the bows, into the landing circuit. Already Little 'F' has conferred with the FDO and agreed which spots will be used. He also has permission from the Captain for flying operations to proceed while the OOW has resumed handling of the ship and is steady on the DFC of 345°. Flyco replies to the formation leader.

Flyco 'Red Formation cleared to slot. Wind Red 15, 20kt, DFC three-four-five.'

He warns the OOW on the intercom:

Flyco 'SHARs slotting in two minutes.'

The same message is passed to the FDO who alerts his directors. All eyes follow the four jets as they come up on the ship at 500ft and break left into the pattern, extend their air brakes and slow down to lower their undercarriages. As they turn left again to approach the ship from the port quarter they are strung out at 100yd intervals, and jet nozzles are rotated to the vertical as speed bleeds off to match that of the ship. On the

Left:
Little 'F' looks out from Flyco as a Sea Harrier edges towards the ship for landing. Depending on which landing spot is in use, SHARs or Sea Kings may hover only a few feet away from the Bridge as they position for landing – there is little room for error!

Below left:
These throttles on the Quartermaster's Bridge console can be used for direct control of the engines, but in practice this is rarely done.

before the Bridge, while the remainder perform one of the Sea Harrier's many party tricks and taxies backwards to the stern park! Each aircraft is guided by a director, and teams of aircraft handlers are ready to secure each aircraft with chain lashings as they reach their assigned parking positions. The forward deck park is known as the 'graveyard' as it is normally kept clear during the launch of a SHAR sortie so that any aircraft developing problems and unable to take-off can be immediately taxied clear of the take-off strip, allowing the rest of the launch to continue.

Under typical operational conditions, the flightdeck runs to a fairly regular pattern. As *Invincible's* main function is ASW operations, she will aim to have three SKJs airborne on patrol at all times. To meet this commitment the ship's nine SKJs are operated in a 'ripple' pattern whereby three helicopters in the air are relieved, one at a time, by SKJs coming out from the ship. Others will be on deck refuelling and re-arming ready to relieve those in the air, and the remainder will be undergoing maintenance or repair, or are available as standby aircraft. A typical ASW sortie may last up to 3 or 4hr, which means that every hour or so a relief SKJ will be launched, followed shortly after by the returning SKJ landing on to be refuelled and made ready. In between these will be SHAR launches and recoveries as they maintain a standing CAP of at least two aircraft over the task force. This will entail the launch and recovery of two pairs of SHARs at approximately hourly intervals. In addition there will always be at least another two SHARs held on the deck at immediate readiness if any threat should develop. Thus the ship's eight SHARs normally will be deployed as two airborne on CAP, two at immediate readiness, two refuelling and re-arming, and two in reserve or undergoing repair. Finally, one of the ship's three SKW AEW helicopters will normally be airborne with the other two as back-up, each sortie typically lasting up to 4hr.

Thus the ship's flightdeck is almost continually in use throughout 24hr of the day in an operational environment. Consequently there are two Flyco officers aboard, both Lt-Cdrs, who take turn and turn about to run the ship's flying operations. In addition the ship's Commander (Air) is available to the Bridge and Flyco during Flying Stations. In his supervisory capacity he moves between the bridge area, briefing and operations rooms, co-ordinating and assisting as necessary. At this early stage in the commission, when the standards of the ship are being set, he maintains a vigilant watch over deck operations. Normally he sits immediately behind Little 'F' and shares his panoramic view over the flightdeck.

In addition to the equipment and procedures already discussed, mention should also be made of MADGE — Microwave Aircraft Direction Guidance Equipment. This is a combined instrument approach aid for inbound aircraft, and a datalink between aircraft and ship.

In Flyco, the MADGE Data Display and Control Unit has a LED readout which shows the identity, range, bearing, and fuel state of up to six selected aircraft. In addition, the Commander (Air) can select a designated bearing (QDM) on which aircraft can approach the ship and also a descent profile. In the aircraft, deviations from this approach track and profile are shown on the pilot's head-up display and the necessary corrections made.

Apart from its great accuracy, the system is also of great operational value as all transmissions are relatively low-powered and the coded datalink is difficult to intercept or jam by enemy EW measures. In addition the datalink cuts down the number of UHF voice transmissions needed.

The reader already may have observed that there are few radio transmissions made in the conduct of flightdeck operations, and that great reliance is made on light signals. In fact the whole operation could be carried out in complete radio silence if required. This has important applications in an operational environment where any transmission can give away the position and status of the ship and her aircraft.

On this Friday morning in the Irish Sea, such considerations are of secondary importance as the flying programme is primarily aimed at allowing the aircrews to familiarise themselves with a new ship and allow the flightdeck crews to

Above:

The Bridge engine telegraph controls. Required shaft revolutions are dialled up on the lower counters. This is acknowledged from the SCR and a readout of actual revolutions is given on the top pair of dials. At normal cruising stations the telegraphs (centre) are set at 'Half Ahead' with revolutions as set on the counters. In this photograph, 190 revolutions have been requested and acknowledged but the ship is still building up speed and 180 revolutions are presently indicated.

practice their routines. There are several more serials to be launched and recovered, and another flight of Hawks arrives for more firing runs — this time managing to sever the cable towing the splash target which is lost astern. However, by 1218 all aircraft are back on deck and when they have all been secured or struck down to the hangar the pipe 'Secure From Flying Stations' is made at 1223.

It has been a busy and eventful morning and as the Flyco team stand down the new Watch is taking over on the Bridge. The ship is now some 20 miles west of St David's Head and course is due north at 10kt. Although the Air Department has had the run of the ship all morning, it will shortly be the turn of the Marine Engineers to show what they can do as a full speed trial is scheduled for 3hr from 1300. This will enable a number of machinery checks and tests to be

carried out, as well as providing a useful calibration of fuel flows and various instrumentation to be made.

Before commencing the trial it is essential that the ship's position is accurately fixed so that a measurement of distance run can be made at the finish. The OOW therefore checks the Decca and SINS positions shown on the chart plot against a visual fix taken from prominent features in sight, including the Smalls lighthouse on the starboard quarter and St David's Head off the beam. From a navigation point of view, the speed trial is fairly routine and so the Captain has left the Bridge, leaving the OOW with charge of the ship.

A buzzer and light on the OOW's console heralds a call from the Marine Engineer Officer of the Watch (MEOOW) in the Ship Control Centre (SCC) amidships on 6 Deck. Checking that all is ready for the trial to commence he asks the OOW to ring down revolutions for 15kt initially. The ship will not go to full power immediately, but will increase revolutions by stages in order that various checks can be made and readings taken from the various instrument displays in the SCC.

On orders from the OOW, the telegraphist sets the required revolutions on the dial above the throttles and a bell indicates that this has been acknowledged by the SCC. With revolutions stabilised there is a short pause followed by a request for further increases to give 18kt, and then 146rpm for 22kt. Further instructions

increase revs to maximum which is held for a long period as the ship's speed gradually winds up to over 27kt and finally maximum power gives just over 200rpm for a fractional increase in speed.

In the SCC below decks, the operation and performance of the four Olympus TM3B gas turbines is closely monitored by the Watch on duty. This consists of the MEOOW seated at his console, overlooking the two throttle operators, who sit facing their controls and a bank of instruments and indicators showing the parameters of the engines, gearbox, shafts and fuel systems. To starboard is the POMEM in charge of the ship's auxiliary diesel generators which supply electrical power. On the bulkhead in front of him is the indicator panel showing the state of the electrical supply system, and from his control console he can operate various combinations of generators in order to meet the ship's power demand at all times. To complement the Watch closed up in the SCC, there are also four stokers on duty, one in each of the two main engine rooms tending to a pair of Olympus engines and one each in the forward and after auxiliary machinery spaces where the eight Paxman Valenta diesel generating sets are located.

With the ship running at full speed, all four Olympus units are wound up to full power — the forward pair driving the starboard shaft and the after pair the port shaft. When full power is not required, particularly at Cruising Stations, it is normal to run each shaft on only one engine as selected by the MEOOW. In fact the whole system is one of supply and demand. The Bridge decides what revolutions are required and signals this by means of the telegraphs and counters. The MEOOW then decides what combinations of engines and power settings are required to meet this demand and instructs his MEMs accordingly. In theory, it is possible for the engines to be controlled directly from the Bridge by means of throttles on the Quartermaster's console. However, this is never done under normal circumstances as the SCC team are better able to monitor the application of power so that torque limits on the gears and shafts are not exceeded at any time.

Back on the Bridge, the ship has now worked up to full speed, although in the calm and clear weather conditions there is little sensation of movement. The OOW has a fairly straightforward task, maintaining the chart plot with the assistance of his Second, and keeping a lookout for other vessels which may stray into *Invincible's* path. In this part of the Irish Sea there is a traffic separation scheme in force where north and southbound traffic is required to sail in separate lanes. *Invincible* is in the easterly lane and the occasional southbound coaster passes well clear to port.

As each contact is picked up on radar in the Operations Room it is given a track number and the computer prints up its course, speed and CPA on the Bridge VDU screen to the left of the OOW's console. There is a steady stream of calls from the Plot to the OOW to request visual identification of the target. In each case the routine is the same with Plot calling the target number, range and bearing, and the OOW swinging the compass sight on to the bearing to direct his binoculars along the line of sight. Almost all targets today are coasters or yachts. One of the latter is sighted fine on the starboard bow and the computer predicts that it will pass within one cable starboard. The OOW immediately contacts the Captain, who is working in his sea cabin below the Bridge, to advise him of the situation and his intended actions (to alter course to port in order to open up the pass distance). This is approved and the ship is turned on to a new course of 350° until the yacht is safely past. The unknown yachtsman, in the meantime, has been entertained by the magnificent spectacle of an aircraft carrier at full speed rushing past him.

By 1530 the engineers have completed all their checks and measurements and the MEOOW rings the Bridge to advise that speed can be reduced as convenient. After consultation with the Captain, the OOW rings down for 10kt (66rpm), and once

Top:
The Marine Engineer Officer of the Watch monitors the performance of the ship's machinery from his console in the Ship Control Room (SCR). In front of him the two throttle operators respond to demands for alterations in power settings in response to the Bridge telegraphs.

Above:
This panel in the SCR controls the electrical power output from the ship's eight diesel generator sets.

this is done the MEOOW reports that he is shutting down two of the Olympus engines. By now *Invincible* has traversed almost the full stretch of the Welsh coast and is presently just over 20 miles northwest of Bardsey Island, with Caernarvon Bay opening up to starboard. Off on the port quarter can be seen Tuskar Rock with the Irish coast just visible in the haze beyond. In this position a particularly sharp lookout needs to be kept as traffic routeing from Holyhead and Liverpool to Dublin can be expected to cross ahead. Indeed, several are sighted, one or two requiring alterations of course by the OOW in order to steer *Invincible* safely clear.

However, the Afternoon Watch comes to a routine end at 1600 as the OOW hands over to his relief and heads below for his 'tea and stickies' in the wardroom mess. Later in the evening there will be more machinery drills followed by another concentrated FLYEX from 2000 to 2359. There is little rest on a warship.

SCOTTISH DIVERSIONS

Saturday

On completion of her flying exercises last night *Invincible* headed north, passing the Isle of Man and the Mull of Galloway to enter the southern approaches to the Firth of Clyde early this morning. It is another clear day, with scattered cloud patches being hurried along by a fresh easterly breeze; in these sheltered waters the surface of the sea is scarcely ruffled by the wind. Although it is Saturday, the ship has a busy programme commencing with yet more machinery drills between 0800 and 1000 after which the ship is called to Flying Stations.

The DFC is 070° and, in an example of split-second timing which the OOW could probably have done without, the machinery drills are completed at 0959 giving 1min to turn on to the required course at a speed of only 5kt. With the Captain's approval, Flyco signals the first of four SKJs off the deck at exactly 1000 and the others quickly follow in turn. One heads off west towards Islay to pick up a party of visitors to the ship, while another heads towards the Naval Air Station at Prestwick Airport for the routine HDS

Below:
A routine scene on the Bridge as the OOW checks a contact reported from the Plot in the Operations Room.

Left:
One of the consoles in the Operations Room. During the CASEX off the Isle of Arran the PWO will take control of the ship from here in order to close on the submarine contact. *LA(Phot) V. Richards, HMS* Invincible

Type 195 Sonar is employed in the active mode to give range and bearing, but can be used in the passive mode when only bearings are received. The Mk V Sea King can also drop passive sonobouys which deploy hydrophones at pre-set depths to detect sound produced by submarines. A sonar signal processor can establish the position, course and speed of the submarine using data from the sonobouys. Passive techniques are currently much practised by the Navy as they give greater detection ranges than active sonar and do not alert the submarine to the fact that it has been detected and is being tracked.

run. The other two – callsigns Eight Uniform Bravo and X-Ray Seven Zulu – head a few miles north of the ship to start a CASEX with HMS *Ocelot,* a conventional diesel-powered submarine.

The object of the CASEX is to give the helicopter and ship's sonar operators some practice in tracking a submarine contact, and to save time the submarine has started the exercise at a prenotified datum. Thus the helicopters quickly gain contact with their sonars which are lowered into the water on a long cable. The

During this exercise the OOW relinquishes control of the ship to the PWO in the Operations Room and he, in turn, is anxious to take the ship north to close the submarine contact held by the SKJs. This is reported as being 14 miles away on a bearing of 330° and so the PWO calls for a turn on to a course to run down the contact:

Below:
A Sea King HAS5 lowers its sonar while hovering some 30ft above the sea. Note the homing torpedoes carried on the fuselage hardpoints.

PWO 'Officer of the Watch, come left to course three three zero degrees. Increase to 12kt.'

The OOW interprets these instructions and passes the necessary orders to the Quartermaster:

OOW 'Port ten, altering three three zero, revolutions seven eight.'

This is monitored by the PWO on the open speech circuit between the Bridge and the Operations Room so that he is able to check that his instructions have been carried out. When the PWO has control of the ship he will use different phraseology to indicate the required rate of turn, so while the words 'Come Left' (or Right) would be used in normal circumstances, he can also call for 'Hard' or 'Slow Left/Right' according to tactical requirements. The OOW still retains 'Charge' of the ship and can override the PWO if he considers that the safety of the ship is imperilled. Thus, for example, if the PWO requests a turn which would cause a collision or run the ship aground, then he would report this and suggest alternative actions. Of course there are times, such as when the ship is under direct attack, when an immediate response to the PWO's instructions are essential and in this situation it is vital there is complete confidence and trust among the members of the team – confidence which only comes from repeated training and exercising in peacetime.

Invincible is now heading northwestwards up the Firth of Clyde with the dramatic peaks on the Isle of Arran only a few miles to port, but at 1027 the OOW takes control of the ship again to turn on to a course of 070°. The ship is again at Flying Stations to recover the HDS helicopter from Prestwick which lands at 1035. As soon as it is on deck the PWO requests a turn back to 320° in order to pursue the submarine contact which is now held by the ship's Type 2016 Sonar. After first checking with Flyco that the helicopter is secured to the deck, although its engines are still running and the rotor engaged, the OOW calls out fresh instructions to the Quartermaster:

OOW 'Port thirty five, altering three two zero, revolutions nine eight.'

The ship heels over sharply to starboard under the effect of rudder and the increase in speed. Further rapid alterations of course and speed then become necessary as a small yacht sails across *Invincible's* bow and then tacks in a determined, if unintentional, effort to hamper the bigger ship's manoeuvres. Eventually the yacht is left astern and at 1041 the OOW advises Flyco

and the PWO that the ship is steady on course 320° at 10kt. This now puts the WOD within safe limits to disengage the SKJ's rotors and shut down engines – an evolution which could not have been safely carried out while the ship was constantly turning and altering speed. However, with the aircraft safely stowed, speed is again increased, this time to a spanking 22kt as the submarine contact is relentlessly pursued. Shortly afterwards, the OOW commences weaving to port and starboard while still maintaining a base course of 330° in an effort to make the ship a more difficult target for the submarine, which appears to be attempting an attack. Other alterations of course are constantly required to avoid several yachts which have put to sea in order to make the best of a pleasant summer weekend.

One of these yachts passes close on the starboard beam and its skipper calls up on VHF Channel 16, apparently curious as to the identity of the busy warship towering above him. With good humour, the Navigating Officer switches the conversation to a working channel and passes information on *Invincible's* identity and tells the skipper to look out for the launch of Sea Harriers later in the morning before wishing him a good weekend's sailing. 'Good public relations!' remarks the Navigator with a twinkle in his eye.

In the meantime, the OOW is engaged in identifying various surface contacts to the Plot in the Operations Room which is becoming confused by the numbers of yachts and small craft in the vicinity. At one point there is some confusion as to which contact is one of the helicopters hovering with its sonar at the dip. Shortly afterwards, at 1111, the second SKJ is seen to turn and run in about five miles off the port bow, dropping a smoke flare to simulate a torpedo launch against the submarine. A check of the radar and sonar Plots, together with a visual bearing from the OOW, will later determine how accurate the attack has been.

In the next 30min the helicopters make several further VECTACs on the submarine contact, each time dropping a flare to signify torpedo launch. A VECTAC, or vectored attack, is made by the attacking helicopter being directed to the torpedo launch position by instructions from either the ship, or another helicopter, which is tracking the submarine in its own sonar – an operation which obviously requires well practised teamwork.

At 1155 the OOW again takes control of the ship and turns on to a Flying Course of 070° to enable four SHARs to start engines in preparation for a launch at 1200. As the ship steadies on course, a Caledonian MacBrayne ferry is observed a few cables to starboard on a similar course. The Navigator calls her up on the VHF to warn of the impending launch and to suggest that the Captain might like to advise his passengers to look out for what is an impressive sight – more PR!

At 1200 precisely the first SHAR scorches off the deck, followed at 15sec intervals by the remaining three. All four turn right across the bows and change to a Scottish Military Radar frequency for a climb through the commercial air lanes in the Glasgow and Prestwick areas. The launch of the SHARs has been carried out in very restricted waters off Saltcoats on the east bank of the Firth of Clyde and at a speed of only 6kt – a graphic example of the flexibility inherent in shipboard STOVL operations. A conventional carrier would have needed to have worked up to something approaching full speed in relatively open waters before being able to launch normal fixed-wing aircraft.

In the meantime, the CASEX is coming to an end and, after recovering the SKJs, the ship is turned on to the agreed exercise safety course in order to allow the submarine to surface off the starboard beam. Normally the submarine will come fully to the surface in order to confirm that all is well before the exercise is officially terminated. However, in this case *Invincible's* sonar room crew are in touch with the submarine by underwater telephone and receive confirmation that all is normal aboard. Consequently *Ocelot* does not surface but only shows her periscopes to enable her position to be visually plotted. It seems a poor reward for a morning's hard work.

On completion of the CASEX the Navigator calls for a turn on to a southerly course and a speed of 25kt. A fast passage is now needed if the ship is to be on time for its next exercise – an

Above right:
The view from the Bridge as the first of four Sea Harriers clears the ski-jump ramp. Note the Goalkeeper CIWS right on the bow.

Right:
Another SHAR gets airborne. In the foreground are the boards used to calculate the ship's course and speed needed to give a required wind over the deck for flying operations.

determined that the ship should be off the southern entrance of the Sound at 1607 in order to catch the turn of the tide at high water and to take advantage of the start of the ebb flow. However, the CASEX has taken *Invincible* well up into the Firth of Clyde approaches and she now needs to sail south, past Arran and Ailsa Craig, around the Mull of Kintyre and then north towards Islay. The total distance is around 80nm and has to be covered in 3½hr, requiring an average speed of 23kt without allowances for tidal streams.

With the morning's exercises completed, many of the crew are able to go to lunch and prepare for

exacting pilotage exercise through the narrow Sound of Islay between the islands of Islay and and Jura off the west coast of Scotland. Although the Sound is deep, over 60m in places, it is only 600m wide at its narrowest point and subject to tidal streams in excess of 5kt. Consequently it is necessary, even in large ships, to plan a passage of the Sound with great care – particularly with respect to timing. Today the Navigator has

a relaxed afternoon, although the flightdeck crews will be required later for recovery of the SHARs. On the Bridge the atmosphere is relaxed and the ship passes some of the most beautiful coastal scenery in the British Isles. Passing round the Mull of Kintyre into the North Channel, the coast of Ulster is visible only 10 miles to port before being left astern as the ship heads north.

After a hectic 3hr, *Invincible* is approaching Islay and slows down to recover the last section of SHARs, Blue Section break overhead while Flyco clears White Section into the Low Wait, 1,000ft above the ship, as the first pair land on and are quickly marshalled forward into the graveyard. The second pair are then cleared to approach and land, shutting down their engines once on the deck before being towed aft. By 1540 the ship has secured from flying stations and the centre section of the flightdeck is being cleared of aircraft in preparation for various sports activities planned for the rest of the afternoon and evening.

The passage up the Sound of Islay will be very interesting from a scenic point of view and will afford a period of relaxation for most of the crew. However, the exercise has a serious purpose. Apart from her normal function as a CVS, *Invincible* and her sister ships can expect to be called upon occasionally to act as Commando carriers in the assault landing role. For this they can carry up to 900 marines and 16 Sea King HC Mk 4 helicopters to lift them ashore. Such operations may well be carried out on NATO's northern flank among the deepwater fjords of the Norwegian coast. Consequently the art of pilotage in such waters must be practised and the deepwater sounds among the Scottish islands provide ideal training locations.

Pilotage in restricted waters calls for a similar Bridge team to that required for leaving harbour. Apart from the Captain and Navigator, there is also the OOW and his Second backed up by the four members of the fixing team manning the four Bridge compass repeaters. The normal complement of quartermasters and communications ratings are also at their normal stations. This team is in place by 1550 and *Invincible* passes her start fix at 1556 shortly before high water, while the southbound ebb flow is due to commence at 1625. Initial course is 310° and speed is increased to 15kt as the ship is steered into the deep

Below:
The scene on the Bridge as *Invincible* enters the Sound of Islay. The Captain and Navigating Officer consult the chart as the OOW looks up to the channel ahead.

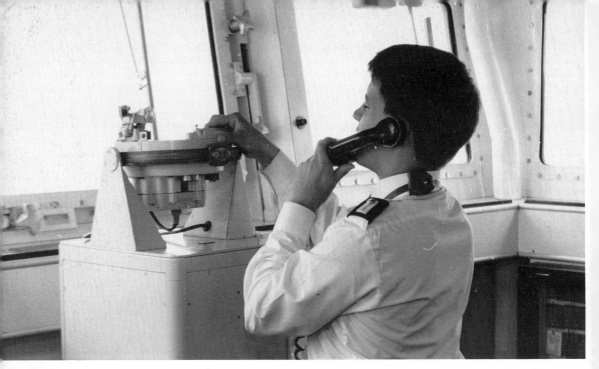

channel on the southwest side of the entrance. Just astern is one of the ubiquitous Caledonian MacBrayne ferries which is also intending to make the passage up the Sound as far as Port Askaig on Islay. A brief radio conversation takes place between the Navigator and the ferry skipper who, not entirely in jest, promises to keep an eye on *Invincible*. Once again the ship is blessed by the prevailing good weather and visibility is unlimited under a blue sky only lightly cluttered with a few puffs of white cloud. The sea is glassy calm so that the ship's wake forms a herringbone pattern of smooth waves spreading out astern. Ashore, the ship's passage is witnessed by the few inhabitants of the two islands, together with groups of holidaymakers walking or resting by the shore. Rising away to starboard are the twin 2,500ft peaks of the famous Paps of Jura, home of eagles and ospreys.

As *Invincible* enters the narrow channel those on the Bridge have little time to take in the sights as the fixing team begins the regular routine of taking bearings on prominent marks which the Second OOW transfers to the chart to give a series of fixes tracing the ship's course. The fixing points vary from the lighthouse at McArthur's Head on the port side, to the prominent Jura House on the shore to starboard, to various hilltops, headlands and small islands flanking the channel. The latter bear almost unpronounceable Gaelic names such as Am Fraoch Eilean, Rubha a'Chladiach and Sgorr nam Faoleann.

Ahead is a green conical buoy, the only navigation buoy in the whole channel, and this is

Above:
A midshipman takes a bearing on the Carraig Mor light as *Invincible* approaches the narrowest part of the channel.

passed at 1615 when the Navigator calls for a turn on to a new course. Turning in restricted waters calls for precise helm orders and the following sequence is necessary to bring the ship round, each order being acknowledged and repeated by the Quartermaster.

OOW 'Starboard twenty. Altering to three four two . . . ease to ten . . . ease to five. Revolutions eight zero. Midships . . . port twenty. Midships . . . Steer three four two.'

Invincible settles on her new course with the Navigator now using the lighthouse at Carraig Mor, dead ahead on the port side of the channel, as his head marker for steering reference. The Second OOW completes a fix and reports that the ship is only 30yd port of track, so that the Navigator instructs the Quartermaster to steer 343° to compensate. Depth of water is reported as 26m and speed has been reduced to 12kt. With small adjustments, *Invincible* continues at this course and speed for another 12min, covering 2.5nm before the next wheel-over point is reached at 1625.

New course is 351° and *Invincible* is now entering the narrowest part of the Sound with the nearest shore only one-and-a-half cables off to port, although the depth of water is over 50m. Six miles ahead, on the northern tip of Islay, the Rubha a'Mhail lighthouse provides a prominent head marker. A few minutes later, at 1630, the

Left:
The Carraig Mor lighthouse is one of several convenient navigation marks along the edge of the Sound.

Above:
The small settlement at Port Askaig on Islay serves as a terminal for ferry services to and from Jura and the mainland. The passage of large ships such as *Invincible* is a rare sight.

ship is passing abeam Port Askaig on the port side and a small crowd can be seen watching as *Invincible* sweeps slowly by. A pipe is made over the ship's broadcast system:

'Warning, ship's siren about to be tested.'

A few seconds later a series of ear-shattering low-pitched blasts echo over the Sound and into the hills, producing a flurry of waves and cheers from those watching by the waterside. It is unusual, to say the least, to see an aircraft carrier in these waters and a sense of occasion is felt both aboard ship and ashore.

Once past Port Askaig, the channel begins to slowly widen although the course of 351° is maintained to keep the ship over to port and in deeper water. At 1636 the Carragh an t-Sruith light is passed on the starboard side and speed is

increased to 16kt. Some distance ahead a small yacht on a similar course is observed and the Plot reports that *Invincible* is catching it up and will pass quite close. However, the Navigator is anticipating a change of course in another 1½ miles and this should then put the two vessels on diverging tracks.

At 1642 the wheel-over point is reached and the aircraft carrier is brought round on to a course of 023° which will take her out into more open waters, although until passing abeam the northern tip of Islay the water remains relatively shallow at around 18m – deepening again once the island is cleared. By 1658 the ship is well clear of the channel and speed is again increased to 20kt, producing in excess of 30kt WOD, although this has little effect on the deck hockey tournament which is now taking place. Two hours at this speed brings the ship up the Forth of Lorne between the Isle of Mull and the mainland. At 1900 the ship slows down to a mere 4kt and turns to cruise slowly up the Sound of Mull while almost the entire crew participate in a traditional flightdeck barbeque. After the activity of the last few days it is a welcome chance to relax as the ship cruises amongst magnificent scenery and sails, literally, into the setting sun.

Sunday

After the relaxations of the previous evening it is an early start for most of the crew as *Invincible* sails into the Minches early on Sunday morning. During the night the ship has passed the small islands of Eigg and Rhum, passed to the west of Skye and is now in the wide channel between the Outer Hebrides and the mainland known as the Minch. Here she is due to rendezvous at 0730 with the RFA *Fort Austin* to carry out a RAS and VERTREP serial which will last most of the day.

A RAS (Replenishment at Sea) can take one of three forms: RAS(A) is a transfer of ammunition; RAS(S) is a transfer of stores; and RAS(L) is a transfer of liquids, mainly diesel and aviation fuel. Today will be both A and S and, in addition, the ship's helicopters will also be used to transfer stores between the two ships using the flightdeck on *Fort Austin's* stern to pick up underslung loads for *Invincible* in a process known as Vertical Replenishment — hence VERTREP.

Fort Austin is duly sighted off to starboard as *Invincible* approaches the rendezvous. As with other major ship-handling evolutions such as those already described in this book, the Navigator will have charge of the ship during the RAS although he may delegate the responsibility to other officers acting under his direct supervision for training purposes. On some occasions the Captain himself will take charge of the ship in order to maintain his skills.

On approaching *Fort Austin*, the Navigator instructs the Chief Yeoman to signal that he is taking charge of the RAS and that the course and speed for the operation will be 020° at 12kt. This is sent by signal lamp and acknowledged by *Fort Austin*. Communications throughout the RAS will be by visual means, flag or light, in order to simulate an operational environment when electronic emissions need to be reduced or eliminated altogether. The only exception to this will be a direct telephone line which is rigged between the two Bridges when the RAS is underway.

Once the RFA is settled on the required course, the Navigator manoeuvres *Invincible* to take station some 400yd off *Fort Austin's* port quarter. Both ships fly Flag R (Romeo) at the dip which indicates that each ship is preparing for the RAS. The RFA will hoist the flag close-up when she is ready to commence while *Invincible*, as receiving ship, will similarly signal when commencing her approach to alongside. *Invincible* has already

Above:

The *Fort Austin* steams alongside at 12kt as preparations are made to pass the jackstay tackle before commencing the transfer stores.

closed up her teams of seamen at the two RAS points on the flightdeck where they are busy preparing the lines, cables and handling gear. The forward RAS point is immediately in front of the Bridge and consists of a short mast supported by sheerlegs with a tensioning block at the top. A deck-mounted winch sited nearby will provide the power for hauling and letting out cables. For the after RAS station, provision is made for attaching the necessary tackle to the island superstructure adjacent to the after Type 909 radar housing. Communication between the Bridge and the two RAS points is by means of an open line broadcast system.

On the Bridge, preparations are also being made. The glass side-port in the starboard wing of the Bridge is removed and a chair on a high pedestal is fitted here. A microphone on a wanderlead is plugged in to allow helm orders to be transmitted to the Quartermaster's speaker. A seaman is detailed to standby in the Bridge Wing to record helm and telegraph orders on a Perspex board in front of the Navigator — an important

task as constant, but small, corrections of speed and course will be necessary while running alongside and it would be easy to lose track of the situation without a written reminder.

Preparations are complete aboard *Invincible* and *Fort Austin's* Flag R is hoisted close-up. With the Captain's permission, the Navigator commences his approach, calling initially for a speed of 20kt to overhaul the RFA which is maintaining a steady 12kt as ordered. This speed differential has to be maintained until the two ships are almost alongside so that *Invincible* will break cleanly through the pressure wave around the RFA's stern, and not be drawn in on a potential collision course. The difficult part of the operation is knowing when to slow down so that *Invincible* comes down to 12kt just as she is exactly alongside *Fort Austin*. The distance which *Invincible* will cover in slowing down is known from data gathered during the ship's initial trials, as is the time taken for the reduction. Distance travelled by the RFA at a steady 12kt during the same time is easily calculated and the difference between the two distances is the point at which a speed reduction must be ordered. In this case the answer is 520ft and the Navigator uses a detailed scale drawing of *Fort Austin* to locate a point near the stern

Above:
The Navigating Officer concentrates on keeping station on *Fort Austin's* **Bridge – visible only 40yd away to starboard.**

Right:
Aboard *Invincible,* **the RAS serial is controlled from the overhanging starboard wing of the Bridge.**

which is 520ft abaft the datum point in relation to *Invincible's* bridge.

As *Invincible* sweeps up to the RFA the Navigator, leaning out of the starboard Wing of the Bridge for a better view, calls for both shafts to be rung to 'Stop' as the bow comes level with the reference point. In the SCR, the MEOOW actually applies astern power to the shaft for a short period. This actually stops the shafts turning rather than leaving them trailing. Already *Invincible* is slowing down and, although still gaining on *Fort Austin*, the relative speed is decreasing. As *Invincible's* Bridge begins to draw level with that of the other ship the Navigator raps out more orders.

OOW 'Half Ahead both engines. Revolutions for 12 knots.'

Left:

Fort Austin's flag hoist includes the pennants Bravo to indicate the transfer of ammunition, Hotel Juliet to indicate VERTREP in progress, and Golf to show that the RFA is the guide ship for the serial. The ball and cone signal shows restricted ability to manoeuvre.

As the power comes on, the ship's de-acceleration is halted and she settles at 12kt some 40yd to port of the RFA, with the two replenishment points exactly in line. With the weather still fair and a calm sea, station keeping is a relatively straight-forward business. By picking a reference point on the RFA, the Navigator can quickly determine if *Invincible* is pulling ahead or dropping back and issues the necessary telegraph orders — usually an alteration of only 2rpm is sufficient. Similarly, very small course corrections are normally all that are required to maintain an exact distance from the RFA. When the jackstay is rigged, markers on the line provide an easy visual guide to the gap between the ships.

Having rendezvoused at just after 0730, *Invincible* makes her first approach at 0754 but has to sheer off almost immediately as *Fort Austin* experiences an alarming steering problem at the critical moment. However, this is soon sorted out and at 0810 the two ships are again steaming in station ready to pass lines. The first to go is a light gun line fired from *Invincible's* foredeck. It is a good shot and the line, laying across *Fort Austin's* bows, is quickly retrieved and attached to a messenger line which is then hauled aboard *Invincible*, reeved through the tackle on the RAS mast and attached to the winch. This is then used to haul the heavy jackstay cable across to *Invincible* and this in turn is made fast to the top of the RAS mast. The messenger line is then returned, taking with it *Invincible's* outhaul line which is attached to the jackstay tackle block. With the other end of the outhaul attached to the winch, *Invincible* can now pull loads across from the RFA while a similar arrangement on *Fort Austin* allows loads to travel in the other direction. Using the jackstay, other lines which will be used for steadying loads can be passed.

A similar procedure has been followed at the after RAS station and, with both jackstays rigged, the transfer of stores can begin. The heads of the Supply and Air Engineering Depts have already reviewed their requirements and agreed the sequence in which stores will be taken aboard and stowed below. First to come aboard will be a stock of Stingray anti-submarine torpedoes for use by the Sea King helicopters, and these will be followed by a full complement of Sea Dart surface-to-air missiles. These will all be brought across on the forward jackstay while the after jackstay will carry Sea Eagle air-to-surface missiles for the Sea Harriers and general stores. A

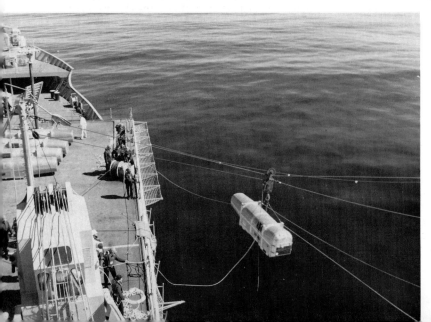

Left:

A Sea Dart missile is brought aboard in its aluminium container. Note the steadying lines attached and also the winch on the edge of the flightdeck which is used to haul in the jackstay line.

substantial increase in the capacity of the ship's magazines has been made as a result of experience in the Falklands.

Operation of the jackstays is controlled from the deck by means of signal bats to indicate when loads are secure and ready for transfer, when lines should be let out or hauled, and when to stop hauling. All crew on deck wear life jackets and protective helmets for safety reasons. The first load, two Stingrays in their containers, is brought to *Fort Austin's* forward RAS station by a fork-lift truck from the storerooms below. Once deposited on the deck, a hydraulic arm lowers the jackstay tackle so that the load can be secured and once this is done the arm is raised and the load swings up into the air. At a signal from the RFA, *Invincible's* winch begins to reel in the haul line and the load sways across the gap and is lowered on to the deck. Here it is unhitched and taken away by another fork-lift truck which will convey it to the hangar below, via the forward lift. In the meantime the jackstay is hauled back and another load is readied.

A routine is quickly established with progress being carefully monitored from the Bridge. Once the RAS is well established three SKJs are readied and launched in order to commence the VER-TREP. Apart from lifting general stores from the RFA, the helicopters will also pick up and return empty pallets and containers as the various missiles and torpedoes are unpacked and stowed in the various magazines. Thus a two-way traffic is set up, the steady clatter of the helicopters adding to the air of activity and bustle. With the flightdeck being used simultaneously by RAS parties, fork-lift trucks, stores-handling parties and helicopters, a high standard of discipline is called for and the FDO has his work cut out.

Once the Stingrays have been brought safely aboard, work commences on transferring the Sea Darts in their large aluminium containers. As each missile comes aboard it is moved forward and then loaded from its container on to a horizontal arm attached to the launcher at the forecastle. The arm is then raised to the vertical, in line with the launcher rails, and the missile struck down to the magazine. A fault with *Fort Austin's* handling gear means that, for a while, she is unable to accept return loads on the forward jackstay. Consequently the empty containers begin to pile up on the foredeck, obstructing the working parties and threatening to prolong the RAS. A discussion is held on the Bridge between the Air Engineering Officer and Commander (Air) to resolve the problem. Eventually it is agreed that the VERTREP will be extended in order to return more empty containers by air. Later the handling gear is fixed and all the Sea Dart containers are returned by

Above:
Once on deck, loads are moved around by fork-lift trucks and other machinery. This vehicle carries two empty Stingray torpedo containers.

jackstay, although the Stingray pallets are still lifted by the helicopters.

After three hours of steaming on a course of 020° the two ships have passed Cape Wrath, the northwest tip of Scotland, well clear on the starboard side and it is now necessary to come to a new course of 090° to run eastwards towards the Pentland Firth. Manoeuvring the two big ships with a RAS under way is not an easy task. After discussion between the Captain and Navigator, and their counterparts on *Fort Austin*, using the telephone line rigged between them, it is agreed that the turn will be made in increments of 10°. After each turn the ships will steady on the new course and ensure that station keeping and speed is correct before commencing the next turn. As *Fort Austin* is the guide ship (responsible for maintaining a designated course while *Invincible* manoeuvres to maintain station) she will signal when each turn is to be made by means of flag signals and a blast on her siren, a procedure known as 'Corpen November'.

Aboard *Invincible* one of the ship's junior officers has control of the ship under the eye of the Navigating Officer and as *Fort Austin's* siren booms out he orders 10° of starboard wheel and instructs the Quartermaster to steer zero two one. As the compass repeater begins to swing round he gives new courses in one-degree intervals:

N2 '022...023...024...'

Closely watching his position relative to the RFA he orders a slight increase in revolutions as

On completion of the RAS serial, *Fort Austin* moves out to a distance of four cables from *Invincible* while the helicopter VERTREP continues.

Invincible comes round on the outside of the turn. As the compass comes to 030° he brings the wheel amidships:

N2 'Steer zero three zero.'

Both ships are exactly in station and so the next turn is commenced while the transfer of stores continues uninterrupted on the deck below. The turn from 030° to 040° is uneventful and the next 10° turn, to 050°, is commenced immediately. As the ship comes to 050° the Quartermaster mistakenly leaves the wheel over in anticipation of continuing on to 060°, but *Fort Austin* straightens up on the designated 050° course.

Suddenly the ships are on a converging heading and a collision is imminent. Sensing the danger the Navigator takes over immediately, ordering 30° of port rudder and increasing revolutions on the starboard shaft to counteract the swing towards *Fort Austin*. Nevertheless, the ships swing ominously close together and *Fort Austin* is forced to turn to port in order to keep clear of *Invincible's* swinging stern. As the Navigator struggles to steady *Invincible*, the Chief Yeoman calls out that the RFA has signalled that she is now steering 040°, as a quick glance confirms.

The situation is still very dangerous and the Commander reaches across to the microphone accessing the ship's main broadcast.

Commander 'Hands to Emergency Stations! Close all watertight doors! Clear the starboard side of the ship!'

Reaction to this is immediate as the RAS crews on deck drop their lines and move away from the edge of the deck. In the meantime the Navigator is leaning far out from the Bridge Wing and issuing an almost continuous string of helm and telegraph orders while a strained silence pervades the rest of the Bridge. Eventually the ship

is steadied on a parallel course to *Fort Austin* but the gap between the two ships is only a matter of feet. Due to the suction effect of the water passing between the two hulls, it is extremely difficult to edge out without setting the sterns swinging together. However, careful manoeuvring over several minutes eventually brings *Invincible* into her correct station and everybody breathes again.

Miraculously, the RAS gear is still in place and with everything back to normal the rest of the turn on to 090° is carried out uneventfully. Transfer of stores begins again while the lessons of the incident are absorbed on the Bridge.

Eventually, at 1445, all stores having been transferred from the RFA, the jackstay is disengaged and sent back to *Fort Austin* while various lines and tackle are retrieved and stowed. *Fort Austin* is instructed to move away and take station at four cables on *Invincible's* starboard beam to allow the VERTREP to continue for another 45min. This will enable the last of the pallets and containers to be sent back to the RFA, a task which is finally completed at 1530. With the RAS serial finally complete, *Invincible's* Captain instructs his Chief Yeoman to signal *Fort Austin* giving her permission to proceed and thanking her Captain for his help and co-operation during the day. This is acknowledged and the RFA is seen to turn away to the west for the long haul back around Cape Wrath to her anchorage to Loch Ewe.

Aboard *Invincible* the crew are hard at work stowing the enormous quantity of stores and ammunition which have been embarked in the last 8hr, while squadron personnel are preparing their aircraft for an intensive flying programme which is scheduled for the evening. In the meantime the ship heads steadily eastwards towards the island of Stroma marking the entrance to the Pentland Firth. To starboard is Dunnet Head, the most northerly point of the British mainland, while to port is Hoy, one of the Orkney Islands. In the bright sunlight and clear visibility the 700ft sheer cliffs of the island and the famous rock pinnacle of the Old Man of Hoy are clearly in view. As the ship decants through the Firth into a glassy calm North Sea it seems impossible that this stretch of water has a reputation as one of the roughest and most dangerous around the coasts of Britain.

After the evening's flying, *Invincible* will continue down the North Sea and later into the English Channel, all the time keeping busy with a continuous round of exercises and evolutions designed to maintain the ship and her crew at maximum efficiency. In the few days which we have spent aboard the ship, she has sailed the whole length of the country and her aircraft have ranged far and wide over sea and land — a striking example of the power and flexibility of the aircraft carrier. The Royal Navy is rightly proud of *Invincible* and her sister ships which today form the backbone of the surface fleet. Already tried and proved in war, *Invincible* and her crew work hard to maintain the operational readiness of the ship and uphold the reputation of the Royal Navy in peacetime. Let us hope that they will not again be called upon to prove their worth in battle.

Above right:
One of *Invincible's* Sea Kings deposits a pair of empty containers on *Fort Austin's* stern flightdeck.

Right:
Return loads are positioned on the flightdeck so that they can be picked up by a hovering Sea King ready for transfer to the RFA.

HMS *INVINCIBLE* - FACTS AND FIGURES

Displacement: 20,000 tonnes (standard)
Length: 210m **Beam:** 35m **Draught:** 8.8m
Machinery: Four Rolls-Royce Olympus TM3B
    gas turbines, two shafts, reversible gearboxes,
    94,000shp

Maximum Speed: 28 to 30kt, depending on load
Armament: One GWS30 Sea Dart SAM system,
    one twin launcher, three Goalkeeper CIWS
    30mm guns, two 20mm guns
Aircraft: Eight Sea Harrier FRS1, nine Sea King
    HAS5/6, three Sea King AEW2. Total: 20
    aircraft
Radars: Type 1022 long range air warning, Type
    966 target indicating, two Type 1006
    navigation and helicopter control radars, Type
    909 tracking radars
Sonar: Type 2016 long range active/passive

Construction Details

Builders: Vickers Shipbuilding & Engineering
    Ltd (VSEL), Barrow-in-Furness
Ordered: 17 April 1973
Laid Down: 20 July 1973
Launched: 3 May 1977 (by HM The Queen)
Commissioned: 11 July 1980

History

After commissioning in 1980, the ship was engaged in a long series of acceptance and first-of-class trials, before becoming fully operational in 1981 when she took part in Exercise 'Ocean Safari'. Early in 1982 she took part in further exercises but it was announced in the House of Commons that the ship would be sold to the Australian Navy the following year. However, the outbreak of the Falklands War in April of that year forced the cancellation of the sale.

Invincible sailed from Portsmouth on 5 April 1982 and, together with the aircraft carrier HMS *Hermes*, provided almost all the British air power over the islands until RAF Harriers were able to establish a shore base some time after the San Carlos landings. During the war the ship's Sea Harriers of 801 NAS claimed the destruction of seven enemy aircraft as well as three probables. In addition, the Sea Kings of 820 NAS flew no less than 3,090 sorties, mostly ASW patrols in support of the fleet and Task Force.

Invincible remained in the South Atlantic until relieved by her sister ship, HMS *Illustrious*, on 27 August 1982. Subsequently she reached Portsmouth to a rousing reception after a continuous record-breaking 166 days at sea. Following a refit during which the ship was fitted with two Vulcan/Phalanx CIWS for increased self-defence, she took part in NATO exercises and visited the USA during 1983. Later she led the 'Orient Express' deployment East of Suez, but was plagued with propeller shaft problems which eventually forced her return to the UK in March 1984 where she was in dockyard hands at Devonport for several months.

The following year the ship was again involved in various exercises including 'Autumn Train' with other NATO units, following which she made a visit to Lisbon. Early in 1986, *Invincible* took part in a West Indies deployment, returning to Portsmouth in March and later sailing to Devonport to start a 2½yr modernisation refit.

In November 1988 she commenced post-refit trials and was rededicated by HM The Queen on 18 May 1989. During the refit the ship was fitted with an extended 12° ski-jump ramp, aircraft complement was raised to 20 aircraft, new Goalkeeper CIWS were fitted as well as new sonars, radars and EW equipment. The cost of the modernisation was around £120 million.

After trials and work-up the ship became fully operational in October 1989 and took part in a major deployment to the United States which lasted into the early weeks of 1990. This was followed by a round of exercises and a visit to Cadiz during April.

The ship is expected to remain active well into the 21st century.

Right:
HMS *Invincible* played a major part in the Falklands War and is shown here at anchor off the islands at the close of hostilities. *HMS* Invincible *Photographic Section*

Below:
The ship visited Australia at the end of 1983 as part of the 'Orient Express' deployment. Note the Phalanx CIWS mounted on the stern as a result of Falklands experience. *HMS* Invincible *Photographic Section*

A recent modernisation refit has altered the ship's appearance. Most noticeable is the increase in the length and angle of the ski-jump, while the ship now carries three Goalkeeper CIWS – one of which is on the bow.

Front cover:
Ark Royal with Sea Harriers and Sea Kings positioned on the flightdeck.

Back cover, top:
Illustrious proceeding through the Solent.

Back cover, bottom:
Illustrious at Portland together with RFAs and NATO warships. *Photographs by H. M. Steele*